JOSEPHINE
EMPRESS OF FRANCE

*

Josephine, the beautiful Creole, who emerged
from the obscurity of a remote sugar plantation to become the most powerful woman in
Europe, has always been the plaything of political
writers. She was, according to them, either the
Evil Genius of Napoleon or the empty-headed
victim of his intrigues for dynastic power. None
of these writers allowed this woman to be herself.

For this, Josephine herself was partially to
blame. She might be dubbed a chronic liar or
merely an inveterate romantic. The result is that
few facts of her life are what they seemed, and still
fewer of expressed thoughts a reflection of her real
feelings. Her age she invariably mis-stated. Her
loyalties and her hatreds changed according to the
political and emotional climate. Her many loves
may have often been genuine passions; they were
certainly and frequently contrived for her own
benefit.

Barbara Cartland has studied Josephine's
bizarre behaviour, her grandiose adventures and
her passionate love affairs in order to analyse the
motives which inspired them. The result is a portrait
of Josephine the Woman, rather than Josephine
the Empress.

Also in Arrow Books by Barbara Cartland

Autobiography
I Search for Rainbows
We Danced All Night
Polly: the Story of My Wonderful Mother
Romantic Novels

Barbara Cartland

Josephine
Empress of France

ARROW BOOKS

ARROW BOOKS LTD
3 Fitzroy Square, London W1

AN IMPRINT OF THE HUTCHINSON GROUP

London Melbourne Sydney Auckland
Wellington Johannesburg Cape Town
and agencies throughout the world

First published by
Hutchinson & Co (*Publishers*) Ltd 1961
Arrow edition 1973

© Barbara Cartland 1961

*Made and printed in Great Britain
by The Anchor Press Ltd.,
Tiptree, Essex*
ISBN 0 09 908100 8

1

'Mama! Mama!'

'What is it, Josephine? Don't shout, and tidy your hair, I've never seen such a mess!'

'Oh, do listen, Mama. What do you think Euphemia has told me?'

'Euphemia! That negro-teller of false lies! I've said you were not to go near her!'

'She's not all negro, Mama. She's descended from the Carib Indians who inhabited Martinique long before we got here.'

'That's what she tells you! She's a negro with a clever tongue which bewitches superstitious fools like your father into believing she predicts the future.'

'Everyone believes her, Mama, except you, and when you hear what she told me you will believe her, too.'

'Rest assured I shall do nothing of the sort,' Madame Tascher de La Pagerie replied. 'But let me hear what rubbish has made you so over-excited.'

Josephine sat down at her mother's feet. She was a well-built little girl for her ten years, with a supple figure which already showed a promise of maturity in the small, high breasts. She had beautiful blue eyes and her hair was a vivid chestnut.

Temperamental, she was inclined to cry at the slightest provocation and now her eyes clouded over at the contempt-uous tone in her mother's voice.

'Don't sulk, Josephine,' Madame Tascher said more kindly. 'Tell me your story—I'm listening.'

Josephine hesitated a moment and then, in a low voice

very different from the excited tones she had used a few moments before she said:

'She told me that one day I would be Queen of France—but that I would not die Queen of France.'

Madame Tascher laughed.

'And you believed such nonsense? Really, Josephine, I thought you had more sense!'

'Suppose it wasn't nonsense?' a voice asked from the door.

Josephine turned her head and jumped to her feet.

'Papa! Papa!' she cried. 'Could it come true, could it?'

She flung her arms round her father's neck and Joseph Tascher de La Pagerie held her close to him. She was the favourite of his three daughters, which perhaps accounted for the fact that his wife liked her the least.

'Euphemia has been right about many things,' Joseph Tascher said half to himself.

Madame Tascher rose from her chair.

'Never in my whole life have I heard such idiocy!' she declared. 'You ought to be ashamed of yourself, Joseph, encouraging the child in these wild flights of fancy—Queen of France indeed! And is it likely she would be found in an impoverished sugar plantation half demolished by a hurricane?'

'Stranger things have happened,' Joseph Tascher replied, but his daughter knew that, as usual, he was weakening in an argument with his masterful wife and now his voice was almost apologetic.

'If they have, I have yet to see them,' Madame Tascher said briskly. 'And if anyone is looking for a Queen in this household they wouldn't choose Josephine. Desirée is the beauty of the family as well you know.'

Her eyes met her husband's over Josephine's head and there was a challenge in them that he could not meet. He turned away, petulantly disentangling Josephine's arms from around his neck as he did so.

He disliked his wife but there was nothing he could do about it. She had not given him the heir for which he longed

6

but she had brought him a dowry in the shape of the Sannois plantation. What was more, she was far better able than he was to manage the estates.

In the manner of weak men Joseph Tascher could only nurse his inner grievances in silence and try to relieve his resentment by playing off his eldest daughter against her mother. He would support Josephine in all her childish pranks, pet her when she was punished and encourage her to defy Madame Tascher on every possible occasion.

But Madame did not tolerate rebels in her family circle any more than she tolerated them among the slaves on the plantations.

'I have something to tell you, Joseph,' she said now. 'Something which also concerns Josephine.'

'Concerns me, Mama?' Josephine enquired, her eyes lighting up. Anything new always aroused in her an almost passionate interest.

'I have decided,' Madame Tascher said, looking at her daughter with no affection in her eyes, 'that it is time you were educated. I have therefore arranged for you to leave here for Fort Royal where you will stay with your grandmother and attend the Convent school of the Dames de la Providence.'

Joseph Tascher stood silent, astounded by his wife's announcement, but in a moment Josephine was weeping bitterly.

'Don't send me away, Mama!' she begged. 'Don't make me leave Papa and everything I love.'

But even while she cried she knew by her mother's face there was no reprieve.

It was little wonder that Josephine did not wish to leave her birthplace, which was a paradise for a child.

'I ran, I jumped, I danced from morning to night,' she said later in life.

She had been born on the island of Martinique on June 23rd, 1763, and was christened Marie Josephine Rose. Her father and mother had been married eighteen months and were in a desperate position economically.

War had caused a serious depression in the sugar-cane industry. A little help came just after Josephine was born when her father was awarded a small pension by the French Government in acknowledgment of his services in defending Martinique against the English in 1762. This money, with the subsequent return of the island to France and a trade boom, might have enabled the family to make a good living if it had not been for the tornado and an earthquake which occurred when Josephine was three years old.

The wind increased to gale force at ten o'clock on the night of August 13th, 1766; at midnight there was an earthquake, and this was followed by a cloudburst. By dawn all was calm but the island of Martinique was in ruins.

As soon as the purple-coloured sky indicated the imminence of a tornado Joseph Tascher had ordered his family to leave the house and take refuge in the only really solid building on the estate—the one-storey sugar refinery built under the lee of a hill.

The big mulatto, Adée, who was Josephine's nurse, carried her to safety, moaning and muttering with terror. While Madame Tascher cuddled Desirée in her arms, Josephine lay asleep while the wind roared outside and the trees on the estate crashed down.

At dawn, when they emerged, practically everything they owned had gone. The huts which had housed the slaves had been carried away by the wind. The palms, cedars and silk-cotton trees were merely ragged stumps. Beyond them the house was a pile of rubble. There was not a wall standing, and the roof was spread over the battered and crushed flower garden.

The only habitable place left was their refuge—the refinery—and there, with such furniture and possessions as could be retrieved from the ruins of the house, the family made their home.

The Convent school was not a good one, and apart from becoming literate, her education did not progress very far. But this seemingly pointless sojourn at Fort Royal was to set

Josephine's feet on the road to the throne of France.

In the spring of 1757 there had arrived in Martinique as Governor a naval officer named François de Beauharnais. He was a man in his early forties and with him came his young wife and baby son, also named François. The de Beauharnais family had originated in the Orleans area, and because the Tascher de La Pageries came from the same district the families were friendly from the first moment of the Governor's arrival. Madame de Beauharnais required a companion and the obvious choice was Marie-Euphemie Tascher.

Attractive to look at but with a forceful character and a ruthless ambition, Marie-Euphemie was soon both the adviser and mistress of the Governor, while managing to remain for a time on terms of close friendship with the Governor's wife.

Partly to assist his mistress from a monetary point of view and also to minimise the more obvious scandals of the liaison, de Beauharnais arranged for a marriage of convenience between Marie-Euphemie and Alexis Renaudin, a young man on his staff.

So determined was the Governor that this wedding should be an ostentatious and memorable occasion that he completely ignored the frantic calls of the French on the neighbouring island of Guadeloupe for help against the English Navy. The island was captured. De Beauharnais was dismissed from his post for neglect of duty and recalled to Paris.

Shortly before this a second son had appeared in the Beauharnais family, and although there was no public scandal about the child, it was whispered that the mother was not Madame Beauharnais but the Governor's mistress, Marie-Euphemie Renaudin.

The one thing which makes this very probable is that when François de Beauharnais returned to France he took with him his elder son, his wife and his mistress, but the new baby, Alexandre, was left behind.

This was just before Marie-Euphemie's younger brother, Joseph Tascher de La Pagerie, married. As he left his home,

9

little Alexandre moved in and remained in the care of the dowager Madame Tascher for eight years.

Alexandre and Josephine must therefore have met as small children when her parents took her to Fort Royal. But by the time Josephine went to live in her grandmother's house in order to attend the Convent school, Alexandre had been in France for four years.

In France Marie-Euphemie Renaudin was consolidating her position as mistress of François de Beauharnais, who had been created a Marquis by Louis XVI.

Monsieur Renaudin had long since tired of his position as a husband of convenience. The patient and accommodating Madame de Beauharnais also revolted against her degrading position and left her husband.

'Madame Renaudin has also eliminated all her enemies,' one of her friends reported. 'Her domination over the ancient Marquis is complete.'

But while she was surrounded by all the luxury and comfort which her lover could give her, Marie-Euphemie had not forgotten her relations in Martinique. She kept up a regular correspondence with her elder brother, Baron Tascher, known to the inhabitants of Fort Royal as 'The Chevalier', and with her other brother, Joseph. She was determined to do something for her family.

The Marquis had begun to consider rather vaguely that Alexandre might get married, and looked among the Court officials, wealthy industrialists and distinguished army officers for an advantageous match.

For no reason beyond the intense family loyalties which were characteristic of the entire La Pagerie family Marie-Euphemie Renaudin found fault with every suggestion and constantly eulogised the charms of her nieces.

'So lovely, so talented, so elegant!' she sighed. 'What chance have they of marriage living on a broken-down and half-bankrupt sugar plantation in the West Indies?'

Her anxiety to hustle Alexandre into marriage seems quite unnecessary. He was at this time seventeen and had not the slightest desire to marry anyone. He was thoroughly enjoying himself with many tawdry love affairs. Josephine was fourteen and her sister Desirée twelve. Even allowing for the custom in the colonies, and particularly among the Creoles, for the early marriage of nubile girls, they were still too young for the plans for marriage to be an urgent matter.

Madame Renaudin, however, wrote that Desirée was to have her portrait painted immediately, and said that if the Marquis approved of it, a proposal of marriage would undoubtedly follow.

Desirée had grown into a very pretty girl. In fact she was so pretty that, in comparison, Josephine was looked on as ugly. It was only human that she should feel jealous, not only of her sister's looks but in having the chance of making a good marriage.

The portait and Madame Renaudin's blandishments produced all that she desired and in October, 1777, a letter from the Marquis to Joseph started on the long and difficult journey across the Atlantic.

October 23rd

It lies in your power to give me your daughter to share the fortune of my son. The respect and affection which he feels for Madame Renaudin inspire him with an ardent desire to be united to her niece. I am only acquiescing in the demand he makes when I ask for the hand of your second daughter whose age is more suited. I could have wished that your elder daughter had been a few years younger. . . . But I confess that my son, who is seventeen and a half, finds a young woman of fifteen too close in age. This is an occasion when a sensible parent must yield to circumstance.

The Marquis was formally apologetic about his son's preference for the twelve-year-old Desirée, pointing out in a lame explanation given in a covering letter to Madame Tascher:

It is not that I have not been told most agreeable things about

11

your eldest daughter, but my son finds her too old in comparison with himself.

As Josephine was more than three years younger than Alexandre the young man was either being gratuitously insulting or Madame Renaudin had already prejudiced him against Josephine. There is no doubt that Josephine already had a bad reputation on the island and someone may easily have hinted to her aunt that she was not the virginal gift an aristocratic bridegroom would desire, and indeed demand.

There were stories of a warm attachment to a young man called 'William'. A great deal of mystery surrounds this figure but there is no doubt of his attachment to Josephine, or that their *affaire* caused a great deal of malicious gossip.

The slight on his beloved eldest daughter was not lost on Joseph. But there was little he could have done about it had not the letter arrived when it was absolutely impossible to comply with its request.

On October 16th, seven days before the Marquis wrote asking for Desirée's hand in marriage, the child had sickened of a tropic fever and died.

Joseph in telling the Marquis the sad news could not help but extol the charms of Josephine, for he still loved her the best of all his children.

My eldest daughter who has left the Convent some time since will be a little affected, I fear, by the preference shown to her younger sister. She has a very good skin, fine eyes and arms, and a commendable taste for music. I arranged for a teacher of the guitar when she was at the Convent and she made good use of this tuition and has a very charming voice. It is a pity that she has not the benefits of a French education. If it were just myself who was concerned I would have sent you two girls instead of one, but how can a mother be parted from two daughters when death has taken from her a third?

There was a distinct lack of enthusiasm for Josephine in the correspondence from France which ensued, matched only by the anxiety to find some means of uniting the families.

It was very obvious that Josephine was not wanted by the Marquis or Madame Renaudin.

Joseph, who could not bear to lose his eldest child, was ready and willing to send his youngest child, Manette (Marie-Françoise), then eleven. But here Madame Tascher protested violently and summoned her mother, Madame des Verges de Sannois, to support her. Joseph's mother-in-law disapproved of Madame Renaudin and her liaison with the Marquis and made no secret of it. What was more, Manette was so distraught at the idea of going to France that she became seriously ill.

Despairingly Joseph realised that it would have to be Josephine after all. He wrote to his sister:

You know, my dear sister, the blind devotion of most of our Creole mothers for their children. Not only is 'Manette' opposed to the voyage, but so are her mother and her grandmother—and you know what that means! If I had but the means I would start immediately with the eldest, who not only wishes to see la belle France, but is consumed with a desire to see her dear aunt. Only two things prevent me; a lack of means and the fact that Josephine was fifteen years old yesterday. She is, likewise, well developed for her age; indeed for the last five or six months has seemed to be nearer eighteen than fifteen.

This last remark cannot have proved very reassuring to Madame Renaudin, and must have merely added to the suspicions she already had about Josephine's purity.

However, she was a practical woman. If Manette would not come she must accept Josephine or abandon her plans altogether. She coerced the Marquis into agreeing with her and, somewhat reluctantly, he sent Joseph a letter asking him to bring Josephine to France.

Joseph, who had also accepted the inevitable, decided to sail at once, but at that very moment peace was concluded between France and the rebellious American subjects of the King of England. France and England were therefore at war and the seas were unsafe.

The journey was postponed and Josephine, disappointed but still excited at the change in her fortunes, went back to her grandmother at Fort Royal.

Here she met a large number of American officers on their way to America, and the time passed quickly.

Finally, in the autumn of 1779, Josephine and her father sailed for France.

The voyage was a ghastly experience. The ship was near to capsizing a dozen times in the violent autumn gales, the food almost ran out. Joseph, bad-tempered and racked with pain, kept to his cabin and, as the weather grew colder, Josephine shivered at night without enough blankets to keep her warm.

It was a cloudy, wet day when they docked at Brest on October 20th, 1779. The letters announcing their departure from Martinique had arrived too late and there was no one to meet them.

'I wish we had never left home,' Josephine cried passionately.

In the same year a ten-year-old boy from Corsica set foot for the first time on the French mainland. It impressed him as a hostile country. His name was Napoleon Bonaparte.

2

Madame Renaudin took Alexandre de Beauharnais to Brest to meet his future wife. It is clear that he was disappointed with the appearance of the pale, shabbily dressed girl who was too ill to say very much and who had grown so thin during the voyage that her nose appeared unduly prominent.

But somehow Madame Renaudin must have talked away his qualms so that he wrote a letter to his father in which he both warned him about Josephine's lack of glamour but found a means of paying half-hearted testimony to her desirability as a wife.

Mademoiselle de La Pagerie will probably appear to you less pretty than you expected, but I think I can assure you that her modesty and sweetness of her character surpass anything that you have been told.

The only person who was really satisfied with the matter was Madame Renaudin. Against every obstacle of circumstance and human wish she had got her own way. She was determined to make everything sound well and wrote to the Marquis saying:

Alexandre is very much occupied at present, very much absorbed with your future daughter-in-law.

The wedding took place on December 13th, 1779, in the little parish church of Noisy-le-Grand. It was a very quiet

15

ceremony and Joseph Tascher was too ill with malaria to be present.

There was no honeymoon; the holiday period for newly marrieds was then regarded as a pagan and therefore plebeian custom suitable for the peasantry but not for the aristocracy.

Alexandre was always anxious to prove his aristocratic bearing. His insistence on being addressed as Viconte began when he entered the army at fifteen. His claim to the title was doubtful, which was the more powerful motive for his behaving as he imagined a Vicomte would.

In fact the young man was disliked in Court circles. Through being in the army and because of his father's social standing he obtained invitations to the larger functions, but at more intimate and informal gatherings his company was dispensed with.

His pedantic criticisms of art and literature, based on imitation of others rather than any spurring of his own callow taste, were infuriating. Even in the sowing of the wild oats which he imagined to be the conventional habit of any young man of standing he lacked the flair to steer between amorous adventure and repellent lust. Unattractive in manner and crude in love, his affairs were only with street women.

Josephine was a naturally passionate girl, but she had plenty of self-respect. It cannot be said that she came to Alexandre as a wide-eyed innocent, but her husband's love-making disgusted her. A more delicately brought-up girl might have accepted that this was the inevitable burden of marriage but Josephine knew better.

In the few short weeks that they were constantly together— Alexandre rejoined his regiment in the spring of 1780— Josephine's chance of having a happy, ordinary marriage was lost. The first thing she learnt from Alexandre was that passion was something quite apart from love. It was a lesson which was to colour and change her whole life and to confound and puzzle future historians.

Alexandre aggravated the feeling that she was merely a toy

16

for his physical amusement by perpetually criticising her ignorance and crude manners.

'You're so stupid, so provincial, so *gauche*,' he would storm.

Ignorant Josephine was by general admission, including her own, but she had an innate sense of good taste by any standard except that of the social climbers around the stilted French Court. There the dimensions of a handkerchief or the way it was held folded in the hand could make or mar the owner's social status.

Under the pretence of instructing her, Alexandre maintained a campaign of sneering contempt which would have destroyed the confidence of any girl without the buoyant high-spirited determination which was one of Josephine's strongest characteristics.

Alexandre also found his wife was beginning to be an expensive luxury and raged at her continuously.

'How do you think I can meet these bills?' he would ask. 'Your extravagance is insupportable.'

He frequently lost his temper, swore at her and even struck her.

Josephine wept copiously. She had always resorted to tears when things went wrong but they only exasperated Alexandre. Unfortunately he found that Josephine, red-eyed and trembling from his violence, incited a great deal of sympathy, which harmed his position among his relations and friends.

'I thought he was a philosopher and a student of Rousseau,' said one of his contemporaries. 'It only shows one never knows the truth.'

After Alexandre had gone away on military duties his letters to Josephine were chiefly concerned with criticism of the grammar, style and phrasing of the notes she wrote to him.

Her letters have not survived but from the incidental comments in her husband's it is obvious that she queried his fidelity. Not through the usual misgivings of a bride jealous because her beloved was far away, but because of the stories that the spiteful gossips took care she heard.

Josephine was fundamentally easy-going; her indolent mind could tolerate in others the promiscuous flirtations that she herself was always ready to enjoy. But she was sensitive to the insult of being on the same footing as some of the regiments of harlots who trailed behind the armies of France.

She turned for consolation to the excitements of the social life around her. Among her close friends there was Madame Fanny de Beauharnais, the divorced wife of the Marquis's brother, Comte Claude, and Madame de Montesson, the morganatic wife of the Duc d'Orleans.

These two attractive rather *déclassé* women taught Josephine how to spend money and whispered confidences of the delights of love. Josephine was an apt and eager pupil.

She learnt, however, that her father-in-law, the Marquis, by his association with Madame Renaudin, was not received at Court. Alexandre had applied for admission of his wife to the official list but it was not granted. He was told the Queen would receive the Vicomtesse de Beauharnais only privately.

Twice, in private, Josephine went to the Trianon. Once the King was present, but she was never invited to a public function.

Her new friends soon gossiped about the unkind and often brutal treatment she was receiving from her husband. Alexandre was furious and his anger was increased by the Royal refusal to recognise his wife publicly.

He blamed Josephine for everything and forbade her to associate with Madame Fanny, Madame de Montesson and even Madame Renaudin.

'I will have no more of these disreputable women inflencing you against me,' he stormed.

Josephine appealed to the Marquis, and Alexandre found he was not strong enough to see that his orders were carried out.

By the time Josephine conceived in December, 1780, the marriage was virtually finished. Alexandre did not trouble to turn up when the birth was near, but took good care to be present in the role of proud father at the christening in Paris. He also saw that invitations were despatched to everyone of importance.

As soon as he could he took himself off to Italy on the pretext of enlarging his knowledge of art. In reality he wished to escape from his wife and indulge in his amours, about which even his tolerant relatives were making protests.

He did not return until his son was ten months old. He found, rather to his surprise, a wife who had gained a lot of self-confidence through motherhood. Josphine was no longer so ready as she had been to acquiesce to criticisms of her mind and demands on her body.

This inevitably titillated Alexandre's interest in her and for a very brief time, perhaps a fortnight, he managed to live in some sort of amity with his wife. In their three years' marriage they had only been togther for ten months in all.

The gleams of happiness were brief, and the fortunate stationing of his regiment at Verdun enabled Alexandre to get away.

He had, by now, begun to brood over his grievances. To Josephine's stupidity and lack of intellectual interests was added a suspicion that she was unfaithful to him.

Stories reached Alexandre that at Madame de Montesson's house she had met the old playmate called William with whom she was on intimate terms.

Alexandre rushed to Paris and found that Josephine was pregnant.

'The child is not mine,' he screamed. 'I'll have nothing more to do with you. I'll bring proceedings against you in the courts.'

Consternation followed. But Alexandre's mind was made up, he was determined to go to Martinique, convinced that there he could find evidence of Josephine's association with William in the past.

He offered his services as *aide-de-camp* to the Marquis of Bouillé, but this was refused. He then offered his services in any capacity, sailed from Brest on September 30th, 1782, and arrived in November.

Immediately on landing he called on Madame Tascher, Josephine's grandmother, and also on her uncle the Baron. He obviously did not disclose to them the breach with his wife because the Baron's wife wrote from Fort Royal to Josephine's mother at the sugar refinery, saying: *I would be the happiest woman, if my own son resembled the dear Alexandre.*

But by the time Alexandre reached Madame Joseph Tascher he was accorded a very cold reception. Josephine's mother had heard that he was making enquiries about his wife among the slaves, and his own behaviour was causing much comment on the island.

He had found consolation from the real or imagined slights of his wife in the arms of a middle-aged woman who hated the La Pagerie family. She fed his suspicions with malicious stories of Josephine's depravity.

When the news reached Martinique that Josephine had given birth to a daughter on April 10th, 1783, a violent quarrel broke out between Alexandre and Joseph Tascher.

'The only war you have made in this boastful campaign of yours,' Joseph accused his son-in-law, 'is against the reputation of a defenceless woman and the peace of her family.'

Alexandre replied with a long list of the humiliations Josephine had inflicted on him and rushed away to the consoling ministrations of his mistress.

One summer's day Josephine asked her father-in-law to come to the room where she was resting beside the cradle which held her two-month-old daughter, Hortense Eugenie. She was trembling with anger, but dry-eyed.

'Read this,' she said, and handed the old Marquis the letter she had just received from her husband.

If I had written to you in the first moment of anger my pen would have burned the paper and you would have believed I had chosen a moment of bad temper or jealousy to write. I have now known for three weeks or more what I am going to reveal to you. In spite of the despair in my soul and the fury which suffocates me I shall control myself. I shall say coldly that in my eyes you are the vilest of women, that my sojourn in this country has enabled me to discover about your disgraceful conduct and that I know full details about your affair with M. de B—— and that with M. d'H——, that I am aware of the means you took to satisfy yourself and the people whom you engaged to help you, that Brigitte was only freed from slavery to bind her to silence and that Louis, now dead, had your secret. I know the contents of your letters and I will bring with me a gift you made.

It is too late for pretence and as nothing is unknown to me there is only one thing for you to do—to be frank. As for repentance, I do not ask it of you, as you are incapable of it. A woman who could embrace her lover after the preparations for your departure when she was promised to another is without a soul and is lower than the lowest of trollops.

You were impudent enough to rely on the sleep of your mother and your grandmother and it is not surprising that you knew also how to deceive your father at San Domingo. I do them justice in blaming no one but you. You alone could abuse a whole family and bring scandal and disgrace on a strange family which you were unworthy to join. After so many crimes and wicked actions what can one think of the storms and quarrels which arose in our home?

What of this last child born eight months and a few days after my return from Italy? I am forced to accept it as mine but I swear by heaven that it is another's; a strange blood flows in its veins. It shall never know the shame and I take my oath again that it shall never learn either by education or treatment that it owes its existence to an adulterer.

But you will recognise that I must avoid such misfortunes in the future. Make your own arrangements. Never will I put myself in the position of being traduced again, and since you are a woman who would impose on circumstances if we lived under the same roof, be so good as to enter a convent as soon as you receive my letter.

21

This is my last word and nothing will make me retract it. I will come to see you in Paris once. I wish to talk to you and return something to you. But I repeat; no tears or protests. I am armed against all your blandishments, and all my efforts will be to arm myself against your false promises, as contemptible as they are false. In spite of all the invective your anger will hurl at me you know me; you recognise that I am kind and sensitive, and I know that in your innermost heart you will do me justice. You will persist in denials because from your childhood you made lying a habit, but you will nevertheless be convinced that you are getting your deserts.

You are probably unaware of how I managed to discover these horrors, and I shall only reveal it to my father and your aunt. It will be sufficient for you to recognise that men are very indiscreet particularly when they have cause for complaint.

In addition you gave M. de B's letters to his successor, and you employed coloured people whose trust can be bought. Therefore regard the shame which you and I, and your children, are about to endure as a divine punishment which you have deserved; it ought to gain for me your pity and the pity of you and all honourable people.

Good-bye, madame. I am writing to you in duplicate and these two letters will be the last you will receive from your desperate and miserable husband.

Josephine's eagerness to show the letter to her husband's relatives was in itself a suggestion of her innocence. She must have been completely certain that their own knowledge of her life precluded any possibility of the charge being true, at least so far as the paternity of Hortense was concerned.

There were some frantic attempts by the de Beauharnais relatives to patch things up. Not because of their fear of scandal—Alexandre's behaviour was too notorious for that to matter—but because they were genuinely disgusted at his unjust treatment of Josephine.

But Alexandre, who had returned to France with his new mistress, was adamant. He refused to meet Josephine or to live in his father's home. From furnished lodgings he instituted proceedings for a judicial separation.

Counter charges were prepared and brought before the Parliament of Paris. Hortense was declared to be the lawful daughter of Alexandre and he was given the custody of his son, Eugène. He was ordered to pay Josephine 5,000 livres a year (about £500), which sum was to provide for Hortense as well.

Josephine, following the custom of wives in marital trouble, retired to the fashionable and quite luxuriosly appointed Abbey of Panthemont for eighteen months. Here she made friends with many wives in the same plight as herself and gained a new knowledge of social behaviour. This she quickly assimilated, showing a natural flair for charming conversation and friendliness which had never had a chance under the hypercritical tutelage of her husband.

Her time in the convent might in fact be described as 'a finishing school'. It was the one thing Josephine needed to polish much that was raw and primitive in her nature.

But the conversation of these women, nearly all of whom had known the passion and thrill of illicit love, was calculated to dispel the last vestige of youthful innocence.

After leaving the convent Josephine went to live with her father-in-law and aunt, who had now removed from their expensive Parisian home to a more modest establishment at Fontainebleau. Life was becoming an economic problem to all the Beauharnais family and Josephine was perpetually worried with debts. In May, 1787, she wrote to her father in Martinique:

I have received the bill of exchange for 2,789 livres which you entrusted to my uncle. Accept my thanks. It makes me hope that you are trying to send me soon larger sums. This will be all the more pleasant for me as they will bring mental peace and prevent us making ruinous sacrifices to meet our obligations. You know me well enough, my dear father, to be sure that if it were not for the pressing need for money I should speak only of my fondest love for you.

I am busy at the moment in caring for my daughter whom M. de Beauharnais wanted to have inoculated. I thought I should not oppose his request in this delicate situation. Till now I have nothing on which to reproach myself. The child is as well as could be desired. She is my consolation; she is charming in face and character. She speaks often of her grandmother and grandfather. She does not forget her Aunt Manette and asked 'shall I see them soon?' Eugène has been in school in Paris for four months. He is wonderfully healthy; he could not be inoculated because of his seven-year-old teeth which are coming early.

This is the letter of a devoted young mother, entirely wrapped up in her children, and speaking without rancour of her husband. But it is also an example of Josephine's perpetual preoccupation with money matters. She was beginning to beg and borrow as she continued to do for the rest of her life.

Money worries were the ostensible excuse of Josephine's sudden decision to visit her father and mother. Without doubt the creditors were pressing; but it is much more likely that the spur to this difficult and unpleasant journey was a much more urgent reason.

The family of Tascher de La Pagerie had developed among its members that tremendous sense of loyalty which is traditional of colonies in foreign lands. Consequently Josephine's activities during her retreat to her parental home after she separated from Alexandre are wrapped in mystery.

But on the island there were stories of an illegitimate daughter born into the family about 1788 or 1789 and named Marie-Benaquette. It is quite likely that Josephine was the mother of a love child.

Years later, there existed in France a Marie-Benaquette Tascher de La Pagerie, a lovely girl in her late teens, for whom Josephine had a somewhat secretive but pratical affection. She made herself responsible for the girl's welfare and means of livelihood.

Many stories exist of Josephine's early love affairs in Martinique. Some are the deliberate slanders of those who disliked her; others the work of gossips anxious to obtain notoriety who enlarged some innocuous flirtation into a passionate intrigue. Josephine was never helpful in confirming or denying these stories. Highly amorous, she was still not the sort of woman who boasted of her undoubtedly numerous conquests.

But there is circumstancial evidence that she did fall in love with a young British officer during her stay in Martinique. He is referred to in contemporary records as '*l'Anglais*', though in fact he was Scottish.

Martinique, after being handed to France in the year of Josephine's birth, was bandied to and fro between the warring nations so that in both 1781 and 1794 it was captured by British forces.

Occupation, liberation and reoccupation were not so disturbing for the civil population as in modern times. A considerable amount of what would today be called fraternisation occurred if only because of the chivalrous conduct of the occupying forces towards the civilian population, and especially the women.

Therefore a young British officer would have been socially acceptable to the ex-enemy, and he in his turn might well have stayed on in a civilian capacity after the island's re-annexation by France. It is possible therefore that if Josephine did have a child in 1789 or 1790, '*l'Anglais*' was the father.

Josephine left Martinque as precipitately as she had arrived. She went, even though her father of whom she was very fond was mortally ill—he died two months afterwards—determined for some reason to put her home life behind her.

The France she returned to was a new country—a land of revolution. Alexandre, with an eye to the main chance, had forgotten his snobbish aping of the aristocracy, proclaimed himself a Liberal and had ingratiated himself sufficiently to become secretary of the Constituent Assembly. He was elected President of it in April, 1791, after the death of Mirabeau.

He flourished considerably for three years, and during this time there were social occasions when he and Josephine met. There may have been times when the desire of their bodies was stronger than their hatred and they resumed their married life.

The insinuations of the Beauharnais family that reconciliation occurred are pointers to this, but they doubtless exaggerate the impottance of what was really a quasi-illicit intrigue between a man and a woman who were neither married nor unmarried.

In the summer of 1791 a big travelling coach rolled out of Paris carrying the King and Queen and their children. Behind them Alexandre de Beauharnais was left master of France.

'I found myself,' he announced from the Chair of the Assembly when the news of the King's flight leaked out, 'occupying by this defection of the King, the chief place in the nation.'

Josephine could not help but remember the prophecy of Euphemia. When she and her children appeared at a window in Fontainebleau the people cheered and shouted: 'You are our Dauphin and Dauphine!'

In the next two years while the revolution—terrible and bloody—swept France, Josephine made friends in high places. She was in close touch with Tallien, Fouché, Madame de Montesson, Madame Holstein and a dozen others like them. This circle was the dregs of two administrations—women who for good reasons the late King and Queen had refused to receive at Court, men who had grown rich by plundering the victims of the Revolution and robbing the nation.

The cry of the people was only in the enthusiasm of the moment, no one really thought much of Alexandre. He had been clever enough to join the Revolutionaries, but he was not one at heart and just as previously his friends and acquaintances had seen through his pretentions to be an aristocrat, so those around him now were soon aware of his hypocrisy.

It was Josephine, however, who put the first nail into his coffin. In 1794 she sent her children, Eugène and Hortense, to the North of France to stay with Princess Hohenzollern, who was awaiting the chance to escape to England.

Josephine did not tell Alexandre but he was soon informed of her action, which appalled him. If it was known that he was trying to get his children out of France it would be assumed that he intended to follow them.

He sent a courier to the Princess ordering her to send his children back to Paris immediately. She obeyed but the mischief was done—Robespierre suspected him and he was arrested by the dreaded Committee of Public Safety in March, 1794.

Josephine, seemingly solely on account of her marital relationship, was arrested six weeks later. Her one-time married status was the only pointed description of her on the arrest warrant, but she had, as a matter of fact, also been indiscreet, not only in bestowing her favours liberally, but bestowing them on people whose political views were suspect.

These included Pierre François Réal and Tallien, both of whom, thanks to their resourcefulness and the swaying this way and then that of the revolutionary fortunes, managed to survive the terror and in due time became very useful to Josephine.

She was taken to Les Carmes prison, a former convent, where she shared a long narrow cell with the Duchesse d'Aiguillon. Although the dirt and lack of sanitation made existence there disgusting there was a tolerable amount of freedom in the place.

Ostensibly the sexes were kept apart, men and women eating in the refectory at different times, and exercise also being under rules of segregation. In fact the hopeless overcrowding and understaffing made meetings with anyone easy.

Josephine occasionally saw and talked to her husband, who was also in Les Carmes. Her children used to come to the gates and send her pug dog, Fortuné, in and out with messages tucked under his collar. There were also intimate

27

sessions in the cell with General Hoche, held for investigation and subsequently cleared.

The Duchesse conveniently withdrew during these tête-à-têtes. Alexandre the meanwhile comforted himself with a young prisoner named Delphine de Custine.

Discipline in the prison was obviously out of hand. Something had to be done about the overcrowding. A solution was conveniently found by charging fifty or so with planning a break-out and these were condemmed to death. They included Alexandre, who went to the guillotine on July 23rd.

He left a letter for Josephine in which he maintained his priggish, if in the circumstances pathetic, attitude to the end. It read:

All the evidence given at the so-called examinations which have been to-day inflicted on a number of prisoners shows that I am the victim of foul calumnies by certain aristocrats who pretend to be patriots and are now confined here. The knowledge that this infernal conspiracy will not cease until it has brought me before the Revolutionary Tribunal deprives me of any hope of ever seeing thee again, dear friend, or ever again embracing my children. I will not dwell on my regrets; my tender love for my children, the brotherly affection I have for thee, must convince thee of my feelings in this respect.

I grieve also to leave the land I love, for which I would willingly have laid down my life a thousand times. Not only can I no longer serve France, but the manner of my death makes me appear an unworthy citizen. This torturing thought does not allow me to refrain from begging thee to clear my memory. Strive to rehabilitate it. Prove in the eyes of all men that a lifetime spent in serving our country's cause and in assuring the triumph of liberty and justice should out-weigh the slanderous accusations of a few individuals, most of whom belong to a class we look on with suspicion. This task of thine must be postponed, for, in the midst of revolutionary temper, a great nation, seeking to pulverise its chains, must ever be watchful and more afraid of sparing a guilty man than of striking the innocent.

I die not only with the serenity that allows us to think fondly of our dear ones, but also with the courage which animates a man who recognises no master, whose conscience is clear, whose spirit is upright, whose most ardent wish is the prosperity of the Republic.

Farewell, dear friend. Console thyself in our children. Console them by enlightening their minds, and, above all, by teaching them that, by their courage and patriotism, they may efface the memory of my execution and recall my services and my claims to our nation's gratitude. Farewell; thou knowest those I love: be their comforter, and by thy care prolong my life in their hearts. Farewell. I press thee and my dear children for the last time to my breast.

Alexandre B—

Josephine was, within reason, very frightened about her own fate. Her migraine became so bad that her face took on a yellowish look and her breathing became difficult. She may have exaggerated her feelings of illness with violent protestations. Anyway, the warders considered her too ill to attend the Tribunal.

One morning, looking out of the window of her first-floor cell, she saw a woman in the street making frantic signs to her. First she clutched her dress and then she picked up a stone. Finally she drew her hand across her neck. She did this over and over again until Josephine realised the woman was saying that Robespierre (robe: pierre; dress: stone) had been guillotined!

It was true! Robespierre's reign of terror was over. Josephine's appearance before the Tribunal and almost certain execution were cancelled. Ten days later she was free. She was one of the first to be released, for which she had to thank Tallien.

Reaction to the imminence of death takes many forms. Josephine's nerve had virtually broken towards the end. Her moans and wailings had upset and disgusted some of her fellow prisoners. Now she was free—and free, too, from her husband. But she was without resources and she had two small children dependent on her.

She lapsed, perhaps without deliberate intent, into a life of almost unrestricted licence.

3

The first love affair which Josephine had after her release from prison ended rather abruptly. General Hoche discovered that she had been simultaneously having an intrigue with a man in his stables, to whom she had been unwise enough to give a valuable gold locket containing a portrait of herself. He also told a friend 'she was always pestering for money'.

There was, too, another reason why the General was glad to find an excuse for terminating the liaison. He had a very attractive young wife whom he had married only a few weeks before he was arrested and imprisoned. While an *affaire* with Josephine, when both of them were awaiting trial, might have passed the time and relieved their anxiety, on obtaining his freedom the General wished to resume his married life without the incubus of a mistress.

Josephine was thereupon faced with extreme poverty. All Alexandre's property had been confiscated when he was executed. Her birthplace had been once again captured by the English and no revenue was forthcoming from that source. Her father-in-law and aunt were, like most of the aristocracy, in severely straitened circumstances.

Money problems never worried Josephine unduly and she borrowed wherever she could, her principal helper in this regard being a French importer named Emmery, who had for a long time bought the sugar from her father's plantation. Although she spent the money thus obtained on clothes and such luxuries as a carriage and pair, she was in a desperate quandary for routine cash.

At this time France was in a serious economic situation and the cost of living was fantastic. Food was so short that it was the custom for guests to bring something to eat with them when they were invited out. Josephine's friends knew that she was so poor that they made an exception in her case, and she was not even expected to bring the bread to eat with her meal.

At one of these social functions she met a young woman, barely out of her teens, who was of much the same character as herself. Madame Tallien was an exquisite beauty who before the Revolution, and whilst still at school, had managed to infatuate the aged Marquis de Fontenay. He had married her just before he was taken before the Revolutionary Tribunal.

His young bride saved her own skin by becoming the lover of the influential Tallien, who subsequently married her. She had many other lovers, the most notable of whom was Barras, President of the Convention and a leading member of the Committee of Public Safety.

Madame Tallien was one of those unprincipled and completely amoral women who had not the slightest compunction about sharing her lovers with her friends. After describing the attractions and importance of Barras to Josephine, she gaily said that she would arrange an introduction.

Barras was instantly attracted. He was not a worn-out old man who could be seduced only by a maiden's body. Josephine's oval face with mobile expressions and ivory skin, the studied languour of her dark-blue eyes with their long upturned eyelashes, her well-rounded bosom, and naturally curly hair delighted him.

Josephine's immediate problems about money were at an end. In the autumn of 1795 Barras gave her sufficient money to rent a magnificent house on the Rue Chantereine in the most fashionable quarter of Paris. Josephine engaged servants for the house, the stable and the garden and furnished it like a palace.

She was, as usual, wildly extravagant and Barras remarked sourly at one party: 'Josephine is capable of drinking gold from the skull of her lover.'

Soon afterwards Barras became even more powerful,

being appointed Director in November. He was a ruthless and unprincipled man who used his position to extort bribes from men and to get women to give themselves to him. Never for a moment did he disguise the fact that Josephine was only one of many mistresses, but she did not seem to mind and she had the satisfaction of knowing that she was at least for the time being the principal and most permanent of them.

As soon as he could, Barras converted the Luxembourg, which had been used as a prison during the Terror, into his official residence. Here Josephine presided over his lavish and magnificent parties at a time when the population of the capital was close to starvation.

It was a very doubtful and mixed crowd of guests who accepted the invitations of Barras and his mistress. Women of social prominence but easy virtue were always there for the delight of Barras, while Josephine found considerable pleasure in the presence of political leaders, generals of the army and such debased aristocrats who had managed to survive the Revolution.

In fairness to this unprincipled phase of Josephine's life, it must be admitted that her motives were not entirely those of personal greed. Her strong maternal feelings may have been equally the inspiration for her lascivious life and it was thanks to the money which Barras provided that her two children were able to be sent to good schools and to be looked after adequately and even luxuriously.

At the same time she borrowed from anyone who would lend her money. Her debts piled up and on January 1st, 1795, she wrote to her mother:

I shall have to depend on your bounty entirely and must beg that you will make me a remittance a least every three or four months.

In October the same year she wrote:

You will receive, then, my dear Mamma, three bills of

exchange, drawn upon you from Hamburg, October 25th, at three months' sight, in my favour, in three sums as follows: £400, £350 and £250 sterling. . . . I need not remind you how necessary it is to honour these drafts. . . .

The money Josephine received at Hamburg helped the situation for the time but Madame de Rémusat says:

Madame de Beauharnais was not well off and her love of dress and luxury made her dependent upon those who would help her satisfy her passion.

Josephine, now thirty-two years of age, was already losing some of her beauty but more than making up for any defects of age by her rapid acquisition of social talents.

A Royalist publication of the period reported:

The fair sex in France, natutally coquettes, vain, dashing and bold, were now much more inclined towards the naked than the clothed system. Nakedness, absolute nakedness and nothing but nakedness was therefore seen at the playhouse, at the opera, at the concerts, at the routs and in public walks, as well as in private assemblies. Where one lady left off a fichu, another laid aside a petticoat. When one uncovered her arms another exposed her legs. . . . Madame Beauharnais, the gay widow of the guillotined Viscount, put on flesh-coloured satin pantaloons under a clear muslin gown, leaving off all petticoats, but at the same time lowering the sleeves of her gown to her elbows. Her long elastic gloves of Grenoble [silk] combined to conceal even her clumsy fingers. Madame Tallien, who prided herself on the beauty of her arms, in turn wore gowns without sleeves, and to distract the notice of admirers from the flesh-coloured pantaloons of her rival affixed borders of large and open Brussels lace to her undergarments.

Inevitably Josephine was making enemies. The friendship with Madame Tallien was even strained by a sense of rivalry, and it was obvious that Barras was falling in love. At a number of functions she became his hostess instead of Josephine. The partial eclipse of the gay widow did not go unnoticed by the politicians looking for opportunities to ingratiate themselves with the head of government.

When the restlessness of the population of Paris resulted in the Convention issuing a decree that all arms must be handed over, Government political police went to Josephine's house armed with a search warrant.

Barras later revealed that this order must have been given without his knowlegde for he claimed that Josephine's residence had been, by his order, deliberately omitted from the list. However, other factions were presumably determined to make a case against her and the agents searched her house from top to bottom. All they were able to find was the sword of Josephine's dead husband.

This was regarded as a good enough excuse that she had been concealing arms and the weapon was confiscated. It was taken along with a motley collection of pistols, daggers and so on from other houses in the vicinity to the headquarters of the young General in charge of the search. His name was Napoleon Bonaparte.

This incident, which might have terrorised a lesser woman, was grasped at by Josephine in a brilliant move to find a new protector. The little General had just been appointed by Barras to the Command of the Army of the Interior with a good salary, a house in the Rue des Capucines and a carriage.

Josephine's son, Eugène, was at home when the police searched the house and as soon as they had gone, taking the sword with them, Josephine told the boy to go to the army's headquarters and demand its return for the sake of the memory of his dead father.

Napoleon was so touched with the boy's grace and his passionate pleas that the sword was handed back to him. Eugène burst into tears on receiving it and there the matter might have ended, but Josephine thought it incumbent upon her to call on the General the following morning to thank him for his kindness. She managed to persuade an *aide-de-camp* to take a request to Napoleon that she might see him for a few moments.

With all the powers at her command she showed not only her gratitude for the return of her dead husband's sword to her son but her extreme admiration for Napoleon both as an officer and as a man.

'I was much struck with her appearance and still more with her courage,' Napoleon recalled later.

Josephine was adroit enough to make this first meeting a very brief one and the moment she saw she had aroused Napoleon's interest she gracefully retired. Napoleon was not one to wait on ceremony and he called the following day.

That meeting was repeated on the next day and the next. In Napoleon's own words: 'The acquaintance soon become intimate.'

What was there about a widow over thirty which sent the blood coursing theough the veins of a young man whose meteoric power could have brought him a dozen lovely mistresses?

As always in these cases, no adequate answer can be given. None of the sirens of history has left a truly understandable explanation of her magnetism. Sex attraction of this kind is inexplicable. Like most of the women who have attracted great men, Josephine's attractiveness was not easily definable or even particularly noticeable. Most of the women Napoleon met socially would have been more witty, more sophisticated, more intelligent. If he had wanted simplicity and ingenuousness he could have found them in a thousand girls of his own social background.

Josephine came to France with none of the genteel accomplishments which were essential to the women of her day. Her father's eulogies about her musical prowess on the guitar can be dismissed as paternal pride. Josephine was not musical and never managed to play anything with even a modicum of talent.

Literature bored her; her interest in art was at first restricted

36

to the desire for portraits of herself and later to the acquisition of any painting purely on its monetary value. She had a taste for beautiful embroidery but no skill to do it herself.

Her appearance held half the secret of her powers to attract men—the indefinable something which makes defects of beauty more fascinating than the beauty itself.

Benjamin Constant, who was Napoleon's confidential valet, has left a wonderful description of her.

She was of medium height with a perfectly modelled figure, her every movement being light and graceful. She almost floated as she walked. Her eyes were dark blue, their large, almond-shaped lids being always half-shut, fringed as these were with the most beautiful lashes; and when thus dreamily she gazed at you, you felt drawn towards her as by ani rresistible force. She had beautiful long, silky hair; its colour—a light chestnut—matched well her dazzling white, soft skin. Yet that which more than anything else lent her special charm was the ravishing sound of her voice. How often did it happen that I, like many others, would stop short merely to enjoy listening to that lovely voice! Perhaps one can hardly say that she was beautiful, but her sensitive kind face, and the seraphic grace of her whole personality, made her one of the most attractive of women.

Her marvellous speaking voice was partly a natural heritage, partly due to the environment of her childhood. All Creoles had an attractive accent, the vowels being more open than in the bird-like quick speech of the Parisian.

Josephine had spent an inordinate amount of her childhood among the slaves and the children of slaves. In those formative years she had inevitably adopted much of the negroes' sleepy, sing-song quality of speech. Descriptive eulogies of her voice are redundant beside Napoleon's own compliment.

'These sounds are as sweet to my ears as the voice of Josephine,' he told his secretary when the troops cheered him.

Josephine's one real defect were her bad teeth. Her small

37

mouth bore an almost perpetual sweet smile and she practised in front of the mirror talking and smiling without showing her teeth.

She also had the natural ability of the Creole to display her charms in any situation and however the body was concealed. It was an emotional grace rather than a physical trick so that, in Napoleon's words: 'Josephine is graceful even as she prepares for bed.'

At the time of transition in which she flourished clothes were sometimes beautiful but more often merely ostentatious and smart. She preferred virginal white to accentuate that dark yet highlighted loveliness. Her gowns, invariably made by geniuses at their craft even when money was short or non-existent, clung to her always uncorseted body, and the first reaction was one of its infinite simplicity.

Her make-up was anything but simple. Josephine acquired great skill in using the cosmetics of the day. She would sit for hours greasing, rouging and powdering her face, trying out a dozen new remedies to hide the tiny lines beginning to appear at the corners of her eyes and around her mouth.

Probably the tragic factor of her life was her periodic ill health. It was rarely serious enough to dub her an invalid, and many thought that her periodic retirements to bed were diplomatic and merely to avoid rows or awkward occasions.

But her headaches were not always social excuses, and give every indication of being the chronic migraine recognised today as virtually incurable. Migraine is at least in part psychological; attacks tend to break out at times of crisis or worry, frustration or remorse. But they are also physical, and in women are bound up with gynaecological rhythms.

Medical science in the twentieth century would be able to examine a woman like Josephine who had borne two children at least, but could bear no more, and discover the reason if not provide a cure.

That the birth of her second child, Hortense, by all accounts normal and easy, must have caused some trouble affecting permanently her ability to conceive, cannot be doubted.

Napoleon was perfectly capable of procreating children and one must accept that Josephine's many illicit amours would have left her pregant had there not been something organically wrong.

This, then, was the make-up of the woman who, in 1795, blithely took the first steps towards immortal fame.

Even though Napoleon was obviously entranced by the young widow, his duties prevented him from spending much time with her. A fortnight after the first meeting there came a time when he was unable to see Josephine at all, with the result that she sent him a frantic note.

October 28th, 1795

You come no longer to see a friend who loves you. You have completely deserted her. You do wrong for she is tenderly attached to you. Come tomorrow to luncheon. I want to see you and talk with you about your affairs. Good night, my friend, I embrace you.

Widow Beauharnais

The request, so discreetly signed in the custom of the day with the surname and title, evidently had the desired result.

It was quite obviously Napoleon's fault, not Josephine's, that they did not fall into bed the moment they were attracted to each other. Josephine was used to men who did not restrain their lusts in any way, and her own passion was easily and quickly stimulated by someone new.

However Napoleon was, at heart, very respectable. At their first meeting he confided in Josephine how shocked he was by the looseness and licence of Parisian society.

'If I had the power,' he said, 'I would turn my cannons next against the drawing rooms of Paris.'

At other times he revealed how his notions of decency were shocked by the behaviour of the very men and women who were Josephine's closest friends.

She realised she would have to be careful and behaved in a

very circumspect manner when they were together, drawing him on, but retreating when he advanced.

On January 21st Barras gave a dinner at the Luxembourg to celebrate the anniversary of the execution of Louis XVI. Josephine was invited and so were Eugène and Hortense.

In her memoirs Hortense writes:

At dinner I found myself placed between my mother and a general who, in order to talk to her, kept leaning forward so often and with so much vivacity that he wearied me and obliged me to lean back. Thus, in spite of myself, I looked attentively at his face, which was handsome and very expressive, but remarkably pale. He spoke ardently and seemed to devote all his attention to my mother. It was General Bonaparte. . . .

On February 9th Josephine's engagement was announced and a few days later she and Napoleon went to bed for the first time. He returned home and wrote to her as soon as he awoke.

Seven o'clock in the morning.

My waking thoughts are all of you. Your portrait and the remembrance of last night's delirium have robbed my senses of repose. Sweet and incomparable Josephine, what an extraordinary influence you have over my heart. Are you vexed? Do I see you sad? Are you ill at ease? My soul is broken with grief and there is no rest for your lover.

But is there more for me when, delivering ourselves up to the deep feelings which master me, I breathe out upon your lips, upon your heart, a flame which burns me up? Ah! it was this past night I realised that your portrait was not you.

You start at noon. I shall see you in three hours. Meanwhile, mio dolce amor, accept a thousand kisses, but give me none, for they fire my blood.

N.B.

A Madame Beauharnais.

Napoleon was consumed with love. It was the first time

in his life he had known the real satisfaction of passion—given and received.

What historians have never been able to understand is the way Josephine made Napoleon so happy when she herself did not love him. The answer lies in the fact that she was a woman who loved passion for itself.

'Do you love him?' a woman friend asked her after she had described her intimacy with Napoleon.

'Well, no,' she answered. 'An antipathy? Again, no. But I am in a state of lukewarmness which displeases me.'

The lukewarmness of which she complained was the reaction between their meetings; when Napoleon was with her she could enjoy to the full the passion with which he conquered her. This was an inestimable attraction to a man who was extremely passionate by nature but had always been restrained by his prejudices.

Josephine was at her best when she was 'making love.' Then she could forget everything but the thrill, the excitement, the fire to which her body responded until a flame leapt within her.

She could not do without this sensation which convulsed her. It was as insidious as a drug, as stimulating as a draught of wine. She longed for it, craved for it, felt that life was empty and pointless without it.

The men who produced these feelings did not really matter in themselves. She was attracted until satiated, and, like a man with a harlot, she forgot them when they were not there.

Napoleon, as a prospective husband who would relieve the eternal anxiety over money, merited special consideration. But there were other men who still had a place in Josephine's life.

Barras remained a very close friend. Many people think that Napoleon must have deliberately shut his eyes to the fact. The truth was that he was too much in love to see the obvious. Josephine told him that she loved him and he believed it. She had for several months convinced him of her purity. When finally she surrendered herself to him, knowing his prejudice against licence and immorality, she swore that he was the only man who had ever attracted her in this way, the only man she had found really irresistible.

There was, however, an unfortunate evening when Josephine imagined that Napoleon was busy and would have no time to visit her. To her consternation when she returned from an assignation with Barras, she found him in the hallway of her house, impatiently walking up and down. There was no chance of lying about where she had been for the Director had sent his *aide-de-camp* to escort her back.

Josephine quickly got rid of the young officer, and then, bringing on the tears which were always at her command, she started her story of injured virtue.

'Before I met you Barras did everything possible to seduce me,' she sobbed. 'He was displeased that I repulsed him and began an *affaire* with Madame Tallien in order to arouse my jealousy. Over and over again he told me that he would abandon Madame Tallien if I would love him. This is the reason that he summoned me to the Luxembourg this evening and asked me once again to give myself to him.'

Napoleon started to approach the door, shouting that he would challenge the Director to a duel then and there.

Alarmed that her explanation had been accepted so unquestionably Josephine hastily ceased to weep. She restrained Napoleon by flinging her arms around him.

'Barras is really quite harmless,' she said soothingly. 'He is rude and foolish but women like him. In fact every woman in Paris is ready to surrender to him! Naturally when he is thwarted and his suggestions are refused he is tempted to physical violence. Darling, why be angry? He has failed where you have succeeded. It is really a compliment to you!'

Josephine completed her reassurances by mentioning a factor which appealed to both of them.

'Barras in very useful,' she murmured. 'I am able to handle him because he does not attract me. You know only too well that you are the only man who has ever excited my cold heart.'

Napoleon was completely convinced. He even allowed Josephine to act as hostess at both public and private dinner parties given by Barras. Womanlike, she made quite certain he wasn't jealous.

'That hideous man! He disgusts me! How could you imagine that I would let him lay a finger on me?' she used to cry if he questioned her. And Napoleon believed her implicitly. Men always believe what they want to believe.

They were engaged but Josephine would not name the day. Napoleon began to realise that people were talking about Josephine and Barras. By now he loathed the man and the mere idea of his loved one's name being coupled with that of the most notorious libertine in Paris made him see red.

On the stormy night of March 9th there was a hammering on the door of the house of the Mayor of the deuxième arrondisement of Paris, the district in which Napoleon lived. The Mayor got out of bed and stumped downstairs. By the light of the lamp he held aloft he saw three carriages pulled up outside and a group of people standing around them.

'What do you want?' he asked.

A man in the uniform of a General stepped forward. 'I wish you to perform a marriage ceremony immediately,' he replied.

The Mayor hastily bade his visitors enter, and his alacrity was increased when he saw that one of his guests was Barras himself. The Director had come along as one of Napoleon's witnesses. Napoleon, with a hardly concealed smile, could not help but glance at him during the ceremony. This, he thought, would show him clearly once and for all who was the conqueror.

His other witness was his *aide-de-camp*.

Josephine brought a lawyer and the husband of her friend and rival Madame Tallien.

The simple civil ceremony provided under the Revolutionary regime was soon over. Josephine gave her age as twenty-eight —she was actually thirty-three. Napoleon wrote down that he was twenty-seven, adding two years to the truth. He was twenty-five.

The hour was late and the weather bad. Bride and groom returned to Josephine's house and retired eagerly to the same bed, where, in the past few weeks, they had already found happiness.

4

The wedding night, spent in the bedroom entirely lined with mirrors, was hardly a novelty for the newly wed couple, but the first hours of married bliss revealed a new Josephine to the infatuated bridegroom.

All her life Josephine adored animals and particularly pug dogs. The current pet named as always, Fortuné, had disconsolately that evening gone to sleep on his mistress's bed. When Napoleon and Josephine entered the room the dog looked up, yawned and then promptly curled up in sleep once more.

Josephine caressed and cooed over it and later carefully slid between the bedclothes so as not to disturb the animal. When Napoleon tried to get into the bed he moved Fortuné, who woke up and bit him on the leg.

'Surely that dog can sleep somewhere else on this night of all nights,' Napoleon protested.

'Fortuné always sleeps on my bed, and always will,' Josephine replied. 'If you don't like the arrangement you can always sleep elsewhere.'

This was not merely unkind but incorrect as both well knew. There had been many nights in the past when Fortuné had been handed to a servant and banished from the bedchamber.

However, the young General who had already shown that he could not be intimidated by friend or foe whether important or unimportant, whether old or young, was ready to placate both Josephine and her pet.

Later, when recalling the incident, he wryly remarked:

'I was rather put out by the matter but I realised that it

was one thing or the other, and the favourite was less accommodating than I.'

He therefore crawled gingerly into bed, keeping near the edge so as not to aggravate the growling and sleepy Fortuné more than he had done already.

This was hardly an auspicious introduction to married life, and in the very brief honeymoon which the couple enjoyed—it only lasted forty-eight hours—there were other slight rifts.

Even if Josephine had been temperamental about Fortuné on her wedding night she certainly did not use the animal as an excuse to avoid her husband's love-making. In fact, now that he was untrammelled by the feeling that he was 'doing wrong' Napoleon became such a superb lover that Josephine never gave him a moment's peace.

So much so that, with the need to prepare a military campaign in Italy urgently upon him, Napoleon was obliged to lock himself in a downstairs room while he studied maps of the terrain where the future campaign was to be fought. Josephine, jealous of his preoccupation, hammered on the door and called blandishments through the keyhole.

'No, Josephine,' he called. 'Love must stand aside until after victory.'

Napoleon had received his orders to move to Italy and he made no attempt to obtain any deferment because of his marriage. Because he was completely convinced by Josephine that Barras was physically repulsive to her, one of his last actions before his departure was to ask the Director to look after his wife while he was away.

At every stage of his journey south Napoleon wrote his wife a letter, the words of which were sometimes almost incoherent with love, passion and adoration. Even more remarkable was that on occasions he even forgot that he had married her and addressed the cover to *The Citizeness Beauharnais*.

Three days after he had left Paris he wrote:

46

March 14th, 1796

Every moment separates me further from you, my adored, and every moment I find less strength to bear the separation. You are the constant object of my thoughts. My imagination exhausts itself in guessing what you are doing. If I imagine you to be sad, my heart is torn and my grief increases. If you are gay and amused by your friends I blame you for forgetting so quickly the painful separation of three days ago. You must be frivolous and therefore are not stirred by any deep feeling! So you see I am not easy to satisfy. But don't be gay; be a little sad, and above all may your soul be as free from trouble as your body from illness.

Write to me, my loved one, and write a really long letter, and receive a thousand and one kisses of a most tender and real love.

Despite the urgency of his mission, Napoleon stopped at Marseilles to see his mother and inform her of his marriage.

He had indeed infringed the strict customs in Corsican family life by marrying without the formal permission of his family or at least of introducing his intended bride to them. At Napoleon's request, Josephine had already written to Madame Bonaparte and this polite gesture, with Napoleon's eulogies about his wife, evidently placated for the time being the misgivings his mother had.

Although she was herself illiterate, a formal letter congratulating her new daughter-in-law was duly sent to Paris. It said:

My son has informed me of his happy union and from that moment you possess my esteem and approval. Nothing is wanting to my happiness save the satisfaction of seeing you.

Napoleon's brother, Joseph, was not quite so enthusiastic and although he also wrote at his brother's urgent request, his letter was cold and formal. No doubt the brother had heard from the younger members of the family who had been living

47

in Paris for some time a few rather damaging details about Josephine's way of life before her marriage.

The questioning and doubts which his family must have expressed merely resulted in Napoleon's ardour increasing, and after he left Marseilles and reached Nice at the end of March, 1796, he sat down and wrote her one of the most famous of his many love letters of this period.

Nice, March 31st, 1796

Not a day passes without my loving you, not a night but I hold you in my arms. I cannot drink a cup of tea without cursing the martial ambition that separates me from the soul of my life. Whether I am buried in business, or leading my troops, or inspecting the camps, my adorable Josephine fills my mind, takes up all my thoughts, and reigns alone in my heart. If I am torn from you with the swiftness of the rushing Rhône, it is that I may see you again the sooner. If I rise to work at midnight, it is to put forward by a few days my darling's arrival. And yet, in your letter of the 23rd, and again of 26th ventose, you call me 'vous'! 'Vous' yourself! Wretch! How could you ever write such a letter? How cold it is! And then, from the 23rd to the 26th, four days without a word. What were you doing, not to write to your husband? . . . Yes, my dear, that 'vous', and those four days, made me regret my previous complaisance. Curses on whoever was the cause of it! May he suffer every pain that I should, had I evidence and proof such as his. There are no such torments in Hell!—neither Furies, nor serpents! 'Vous!' 'Vous' indeed! What will it be in a fortnight's time? My soul is sad; my heart is in chains, and I imagine things that terrify me. . . . You do not love me as you did; you will console yourself elsewhere. One day you will love me no more: tell me so, then I shall at least know how to deserve the misfortune. . . . Goodbye, my wife, my tormentor, my happiness, the hope and soul of my life, whom I love, whom I fear, the source of feelings which make me as gentle as Nature herself, and of impulses under which I am as catastrophic as a thunderbolt. I do not ask you to love me forever, or to be faithful to me, but simply . . . to tell me the truth, to be entirely frank with me. The day on which you say to me: 'I love you less', will be the last of my love, or of my life. Had I a heart so base as to love without return, I would tear it to pieces with my teeth. Josephine! Josephine! Do you remember what I have sometimes said to you—that Nature has made my soul resolute and strong, whilst yours she has constructed of lace and gauze? Do you love me no more? Forgive me, soul of my life. My mind is intent upon vast plans. My heart, utterly engrossed with you, has fears that make me miserable . . . I am bored, because I cannot be saying: 'Josephine.' I am waiting for you to write.

Unfortunately Josephine's replies are lost. Comments in the subsequent correspondence from Napoleon indicate, however, that at this early stage of her marriage she did, at least, reply occasionally. This wifely duty was invariably ignored in later years until the threats, pleadings and reproaches from her distraught husband made her put pen to paper. Then she sent him a brief and usually level-headed missive dealing with monetary worries and giving facile excuses for her neglect.

In the spring of 1796 she was apparently capable of reciprocating at least to some extent the passionate phrasing of Napoleon. But, as the first few lines of the answer from Napoleon in a letter dated April 3rd shows her words were designed to inflame her husband's passion.

3rd April, 1796
I have had all your letters, but none has affected me like the last. Darling, do you think what you are doing when you write to me in such terms? Do you suppose my position is not so painful already, that you must pile regret upon regret, and reduce my soul to distraction? The way you write! The feelings you describe! They are flames that scorch my poor heart. Away from you, my one and only Josephine, there is no pleasure in life: away from you, the world is a desert in which I am all alone, without even the solace of expressing my feelings. You

have robbed me of more than my heart ; all my thoughts are about you alone. Whenever I am bored and worried with business, whenever I am troubled as to how things will turn out, whenever I am disappointed with mankind, and feel inclined to curse the day I was born, I put my hand to my heart: there throbs your likeness; I have but to look at it, and my love is perfect happiness, and there is pleasure in every prospect but that of long absence from my beloved.

What art did you learn to captivate my faculties, to absorb all my character into yourself? It is a devotion, dearest, which will end only with my life. 'He lived for Josephine': there is my epitaph. I strive to be near you: I am nearly dead with desire for your presence. It is madness! I cannot realise that I am getting further and further away from you. So many regions and countries part us asunder! How long it will be before you read these characters, these imperfect utterings of a troubled heart, of which you are queen! Ah! wife that I adore. I cannot tell what lot awaits me ; only that, if it keeps me any longer away from you, it will be insupportable, beyond what bravery can bear. There was a time when I prided myself on my courage; and sometimes, at the sight of misfortunes that fate might have in store for me, I would face in imagination unheard of ills, without a frown, without a feeling of surprise. But nowadays the mere thought that my Josephine may be unwell, or that she might be taken ill—above all the cruel possibility that she may not love me as she did—wounds my heart, arrests my blood, and makes me so sad and despondent that I am robbed even of the courage of anger and despair.

Once I would tell myself that to die without regret is to be safe from any harm the world can inflict: but now the thought of dying without the certainty of your love is like the torments of Hell, the very image of utter annihilation. I experience all the feelings of a drowning man.

My perfect comrade, whom fate has allotted to make life's painful journey at my side! The day when I lose your heart, Nature will lose for me all her warmth and vegetation. . . . I cannot go on, dearest; my soul is so sad, my mind overburdened,

*my body tired out. Men bore me. I could hate them all; for they
separate me from my love.*

*I am at Port-Maurice, near Oneille. I shall be at Albenga
to-morrow. Both armies are on the move; we are trying to
outwit one another. May the cleverer man win, I like Beaulieu:
he manœuvres well: he is a better soldier than his predecessor.
I shall beat him, I hope, and in the grand manner. Don't be
worried about me. Love me as you love your eyes. No, that is not
enough: love me as you love yourself—and not yourself only,
but your thoughts, your mind, your life, your all. Darling, I'm
raving, forgive me. Nature is a poor recompense for such
feelings as mine, or for the man you love.*

Bonaparte

*Remember me very kindly to Barras, Sucy, and Mme Tallien.
give Mme Chateau-Renard my kind regards. My love to Eugène
and Hortense. Good-bye, good-bye. I am going to bed—alone: I
shall sleep—without you by my side. Please let me go to sleep.
Night after night I feel you in my arms: it is such a happy
dream: but, alas, it is not yourself!*

Josephine was bearing the separation from her husband
extremely well. She was seen at even more social functions
than in the past and indeed received far more invitations
than ever. As the wife of the Commander of the French
armies in Italy her prestige was infinitely greater than it
had been as the mistress of Barras.

With a reasonable income provided by Napoleon, no
worries about the education of her children, she launched
herself into a life of continual gaiety, invariably accompanied
by the pretty Madame Tallien.

At the time Paris had a rage for fancy-dress parties. At one
of the most popular guests came dressed as if they were
members of the aristocracy in the roughly made shifts
provided by the prison authorities for their journey to the
guillotine.

Josephine, who had worn this shift and had escaped

execution only by a matter of hours, could find no enthusiasm for this party. But she loved those when the order was for everyone to appear as classical gods and goddesses.

Madame Tallien, whose body was as beautiful as her face, always favoured the role of Diana, wearing an animal skin which hardly reached to her thighs and only partially covered her bosom.

Josephine, whose figure by now was fuller but still had the sinuousness of the Creole, favoured the more conventional robes worn by goddesses in Greek statues. She always took care that these were of the most diaphanous material and invariably white, so that the almond colour of her skin showed through them.

All this time the stream of letters continued to arrive from Italy and as soon as Napoleon had settled in his headquarters he wrote begging her to come to him. When she completely ignored the invitation he changed it to a command.

Still this had no effect on Josephine, who was enjoying herself far too much in Paris. She used to show the letters to her men and women friends commenting with a giggle: 'Bonaparte is such a funny little man!'

The series of military triumphs which Napoleon achieved in Italy astonished her. She heard with genuine surprise that he had covered himself with glory.

Finally Napoleon sent his brother, Joseph, to Paris ostensibly with official despatches for the Government but, in fact, to get him to persuade Josephine to come to Italy.

You must return with him, do you understand. Be ready if you don't mind. My dear, he will see you, he will breathe on your temples; perhaps you will accord him the unique and priceless favour of kissing your cheek, and I, I shall be alone and very far away: but you are about to come, are you not? You will soon be beside me, on my breast, in my arms, mouth to mouth.

Take wings. Come quickly. But travel gently. The way is long, bad, fatiguing. If you should be overturned, or be taken ill, if fatigued—go gently, my beloved.

Joseph soon found the opportunity to have a talk with his sister-in-law and the fact that he achieved nothing by it was a further reason for disliking her, he having already made up his mind to do so even before he had met Napoleon and heard about the marriage. It was not lost on Joseph that at every official occasion celebrating the victories in Italy the wife of the General responsible for these triumphs was receiving all the glory. She was also managing at the same time to parade her considerable friendships for the important personalities of the capital.

Josephine wept with annoyance to think she must leave Paris. She was being a great success—and people paid more attention to her than Madame Tallien. She wrote to Napoleon and said she was pregnant.

New victories were announced every day. If Josephine showed herself at the window the huge crowd outside her house shouted the name that Paris had bestowed on her— 'Our Lady of Victories'.

On May 9th there was a magnificent ceremony at the Luxembourg when standards captured from the Austrians at the battle of Montenotte were displayed. Junot, a twenty-five-year-old General in Napoleon's army, had come from Italy with these trophies, and as the military representative of Napoleon it was reasonable enough that he should stand beside his superior's wife during the ceremony.

Josephine had a role of her own at this affair, for she was one of the three Queens of Beauty who appeared, the others being Madame Tallien and Madame Récamier. Beside these two notable beauties of France Josephine must have looked rather ordinary, but she was quite oblivious of it. She had eyes only for the tall and handsome young General in his full-dress uniform of the Bercheny Hussars.

When the ceremony was over Junot gave his arm to Josephine, who clung closely to him, clasping the arm he held with her other hand. But to her chagrin Madame Tallien hurried up and took Junot's other arm and they walked out into the street together.

The talk about this affair reached such proportions that Josephine's friends advised her urgently that she must go to Italy if she was to avoid a real scandal. Josephine solved this problem by falling ill.

It was doubtless the convenient malady from which she always suffered at times of crisis but this, with the news that she was with child, aroused Napoleon to a frenzy.

He sent a stream of letters to his brother begging him to ascertain what was the matter and in the same sentence urging him to put Josephine in a coach and send it straight away south. To Josephine he sent frantic pleas that she would write to him.

She skimmed through the letter.

Your illness! That is what occupies me night and day. Without appetite, without sleep, without care for my friends, for glory, for fatherland, you, you alone—the rest of the world exists no more for me . . . my heart has no recess into which you have not seen, no thoughts which are not subordinate to yours; that my strength, my powers, my spirit are all yours; that my soul is in your body.

Pages later he wrote:

There is a magnetic fluid between people who love one another —you know perfectly well that I could not endure a rival, much less go on enduring him.

Josephine skipped this page and read:

But I am sure and proud of your love. . . . A thousand kisses on your eyes, your lips, your tongue, your heart. Most charming of your sex, what is your power over me?

His last paragraph made her laugh:

Do you remember my dream in which I was your boots, your

dress, and in which I made you come bodily into my heart?
Why has not Nature arrranged matters in this way? She has
much to accomplish yet.

Josephine showed this to her friends.

'*Il est drole, Bonaparte!*' she giggled.

Josephine meant to write but the days were so full and
writing was such an effort. Another missive arrived from
Napoleon—it was bitter and reproachful. Sentences seemed
to jump out of the paper when Josephine read it.

Bologna, June 20, 1796

You were to have left Paris on the 5th. You were to have left
on the 11th. You had not left on the 12th. My soul had been
filled with joy. It is filled with pain. . . . My heart never felt
anything mediocre; it denied itself love. You inspired it with a
boundless passion—a frenzy which degraded it. . . . Cruel one,
why have you led me to place hope in a feeling that you do not
possess? But reproaches are unworthy of me. I have never
believed in happiness. . . . Adieu, Josephine. Remain in Paris.
Do not write me any more. But at least respect my hearth. A
thousand daggers tear my soul; do not drive them in any
further. Adieu, my happiness, my love, everything that existed
for me on earth!

Bonaparte

Josephine felt uneasy. She wrote him a letter of three lines
and actually managed to find time for another of some
length a week later.

Napoleon in this time completed the conquest of Italy and
received the submission of the Pope. From Pistoria he wrote,
on June 26th:

You ought to have started on May 22. Being good-natured, I
waited till June 1, as if a pretty woman would give up her habits,
her friends, both Madame Tallien and a dinner with Barras, and
the acting of a new play, and Fortuné—yes, Fortuné whom you

55

*love much more than your husband, for whom you have only
a little of the liking and a share of the easy benevolence with
which your heart abounds. Every day I count up your misdeeds.
I lash myself to fury in order to love you no more. But don't I
love you the more? In fact, my peerless little mother, I will tell
you my secret. Set me at defiance, stay in Paris, have lovers—let
everybody know it—never write me a monosyllable! Then I shall
love you ten times more for it; and it is not folly, a delirious
fever, and I shall not get the better for it. Oh! would Heaven
I could get better. But don't tell me you are ill. Don't try to
justify yourself. Good heavens! you are pardoned.*

Josephine consulted her friends. She wept bitterly when they
all, including Barras, advised her to go to Italy.

'Poor woman,' one of them remarked. 'Her grief was
extreme and when she saw there was no means of escape she
burst into tears and sobbed as if she were going to the guillotine.'

On the night before her departure Josephine had dinner for
the last time with Barras and the next morning set off for
Milan.

She did not intend to be lonely on the journey. It was
almost an expedition which rumbled along the cobbles of the
French capital shortly after dawn on a fine June morning.
Joseph Bonaparte was there at his brother's request to look
after her, as well as her personal maid, Louise, three servants
(one of whom was made responsible for the pug dog, Fortuné),
and Generals Junot and Murat.

Junot, at Josephine's special request, travelled slowly in the
coaches instead of riding post-haste back to his military duties.
They were not very far on their journey before she had
wished that she had not done so. For the young General, who
was becoming more and more alarmed about the intimacy he
enjoyed with his superior's wife, adroitly solved the problem
by starting an affair with the maidservant, Louise.

Josephine, who was always a fatalist, did not lose her
temper about this even though she did find an excuse to

dismiss the maid at the end of the journey. Instead she comforted herself by looking on Murat with greater favour.

The two had flirted in a mild sort of way, as was the habit of most of the society of that time, in the previous weeks in Paris, but on this journey they became intimate. The affair continued for a time after Josephine's arrival in Italy.

The party reached Milan on June 29th. Napoleon had installed himself at the Serbollini Palace but he was not there. Instead she found a note sending her a thousand kisses and telling her he was in bed at Roverbella. Josephine was not concerned as Murat was only too ready to fill his place.

The conqueror arrived two days later looking pale and worn but full of fire and abject devotion. Josephine was exhausted by love all night and public appearances all day.

They rushed from banquet to banquet, they received a thousand people every day, her hand was worn away with kisses, the cheering crowds began to give her a headache.

The military situation grew so serious that Napoleon was compelled against all his personal desires to leave Josephine and once again his ardent letters began to stream from his military headquarters to the Serbollini Palace.

Marmirolo, July 17th
9 p.m.

Ever since I left you I have been sad—I am only happy by your side. Ceaselessly I recall your kisses, your tears, your enchanting jealously. . . . I thought I loved you some days ago but since I saw you I feel that I love you a thousand times more. . . . Ah, pray let me see some of your faults; be less beautiful, less gracious, less tender and especially, less kind; above all, never be jealous, never weep, your tears madden me, fire my blood. Millions of kisses, and even to Fortuné, in spite of his naughtiness.

The next day his letter written at 2 p.m., ended:

A thousand kisses as burning as you are cold.

On July 19th he said:

Achilles has just ridden post from Milan; no letters from my beloved! Adieu, my unique joy. When will you be able to rejoin me? I shall have to fetch you myself from Milan.
A thousand kisses as fiery as my soul, as chaste as yourself.

From Castiglione on July 22nd Napoleon wrote that he had made every arrangement for Josephine to join him. She had begged him to come to her but the new Austrian army was attacking in strength and his troops had not been reinforced.

The needs of the army require my presence hereabouts, he wrote, *it is impossible that I can leave it to come to Milan. . . . I beg you therefore to come to Brescia. I am sending Murat to prepare apartments for you there in the town.*

Josephine was forced on the road again. But when she joined Bonaparte at Brescia on July 25th, she found only gloom and anxiety, for the Austrians were pressing him hard. She grumbled and complained and said the guns gave her headaches.

On July 29th Josephine's carriage was nearly captured in an Austrian ambuscade. She escaped only by the skin of her teeth.

Napoleon had gone to Verona to retrieve the military position and had sent Josephine with an escort of cavalry to Milan along the shores of Lake Garda. Some Austrians in a boat on the lake opened fire. Two horses of her coach were killed and she had to run across some fields until a farm cart was commandeered to take her to safety.

Napoleon met her at Castiglione and told her that the enemy had, for the time being, cut off all the routes to Milan. Near Verona they were involved in a skirmish and a number of their bodyguard were wounded.

Just as had occurred when Josephine was in prison during

the Terror, her nerve broke. She cried and screamed and fainted dead away.

'The enemy will pay heavily for this,' Napoleon vowed.

Hysterically, Josephine refused to stay another moment and Napoleon was forced to send her to Lucca. There the Senate waited on her and made her a present of their sacred oil which was especially kept for Royalty.

Josephine was not interested. Terrified and exhausted, all she wanted to do was to get away from the noise, the smell and the danger. She went to Florence; then started for Milan, expecting every day to be told of Napoleon's defeat.

'He's over-reached himself,' she told those who accompanied her, not once but a thousand times.

When she entered Milan the bells were ringing wildly and continued to do so for five days. Napoleon had broken the second Austrian army.

He wrote to his wife on August 30th:

You cannot imagine my uneasiness. I left you vexed, annoyed, and not well.

A letter which Josephine wrote to the Marquise de Beauharnais (her aunt had at long last married the Marquis) is significant of her mental attitude at this period.

Monsieur Serbolloni will inform you how I have been received in Italy, fêted wherever I went. While I prefer to be just a nobody in France, I do not care for the honours of this country. I am very weary. My state of health contributes much to my misery. I am often ill.

There was, for the time being, no chance of her being allowed to return to Paris. For one thing the journey was too dangerous and, secondly, Napoleon had put his foot down about it.

He wrote his wife unhappy letters:

To be parted is dreadful, the nights are long, stupid and wearisome; the day's work is monotonous.

Far from you I cannot live, the happiness of my life is near my gentle Josephine. Think of me!

I write very often and you seldom. You are naughty and undutiful. . . . Adieu, charming Josephine: one of these nights the door will be burst open with a bang as if by a jealous husband and, in a moment, I shall be in your arms.

Your letters are cold as if you were fifty; we might have been married fifteen years.

Josephine was bored with Milan and Napoleon's letters. She looked for someone to comfort her in her loneliness. She found the man she wanted in a young officer named Hippolyte Charles, who had by political and social influence become an Assistant Adjutant General.

He was not a fighting man and preferred to remain in the safety of the army's rear organising supplies. He was a small man of dark complexion with black hair and an elegance which was almost effeminate. His principal social attribute was a flair for making puns and weak jokes in a mincing and precious accent which infuriated most people but seemed to delight the essentially simple mind of Josephine.

To get away from the criticism of Napoleon's friends and colleagues in Milan Josephine found an excuse to go off to Genoa. Hippolyte Charles soon followed her, allegedly on military business.

The French had been completely victorious at the second battle of Arcole on November 17th. On the 18th Napoleon re-entered Verona, having left it in full retreat on the night of the 14th. He wrote to Josephine:

Verona, November 19th. Noon
My adored Josephine—Once more I breathe freely. Death is

*no longer before me, and glory and honour are once more re-
established. . . . We have made five thousand prisoners, and
killed at least six thousand of the enemy. . . . If you cease to love
your Achilles, if for him your heart grows cold, you will be very
cruel, very unjust. But I am sure you will always remain my
faithful mistress, as I shall ever remain your fond lover. Death
alone can break the chain which sympathy and sentiment have
forged.*

Four days later he wrote again sarcastically but not really
for one moment believing what he wrote.

Verona, November 23rd, 1796

*I don't love you an atom; on the contrary, I detest you. You
are a good for nothing, very ungraceful, very tactless, very
tatterdemalion. You never write to me, you don't care for your
husband; you know the pleasure your letters give him, and
you write him barely half-a-dozen lines, thrown off anyhow.*

*How, then, do you spend the livelong day, madam? What
business of such importance robs you of the time to write to
your very kind lover? What inclination stifles and alienates love,
the affectionate and unvarying love which you promised me?
Who may this paragon be, this new lover who engrosses all your
time, is master of your days, and prevents you from concerning
yourself about your husband? Josephine, be vigilant; one fine
night the doors will be broken in, and I shall be before
you.*

*Truly, my dear, I am uneasy at getting no news from you.
Write me four pages immediately, and some of those charming
remarks which fill my heart with the pleasures of imagination.*

*I hope that before long I shall clasp you in my arms, and cover
you with a million kisses as burning as if under the equator.*

Bonaparte

On November 27th, still not having heard from Josephine,
Napoleon rode to Milan. He arrived at the palace impatient,
uneasy, reproachful only to find her gone! Filled with bitter-

ness and disappointment he dashed off a letter to her at Genoa.

Milan, November 27th, 1796
3 p.m.

I get to Milan; I fling into your room; I have left all in order to see you, to clasp you in my arms. . . . You were not there. You gad about the towns amid junketings; you run farther from me when I am at hand; you care no longer for your dear Napoleon. A passing fancy made you love him; fickleness renders him indifferent to you.

Used to perils, I know the remedy for weariness and the ills of life. The ill-luck that I now suffer is past all calculations; I did right not to anticipate it.

I shall be here till the evening of the 29th. Don't alter your plans; have your fling of pleasure; happiness was invented for you. The whole world is only too happy if it can please you, and only your husband is very, very unhappy.

Bonaparte

The next morning at 8 a.m., before Josephine could have received his previous letter, he wrote again:

I am of no consequence, either the happiness or the misery of a man whom you don't love is a matter of no moment. . . . When I exacted from you a love like my own I was wrong; why expect lace to weigh as heavy as gold? When I sacrifice to you all my desires, all my thoughts, every moment of my life, I obey the sway which your charms, your disposition, and your whole personality have so effectively exerted over my unfortunate heart. . . .

Farewell, beloved wife; farewell, my Josephine. . . . I will hide my profound grief. . . .

I reopen my letter to give you a kiss. . . . Ah! Josephine!. . . Josephine!

Bonaparte

On receiving these letters Josephine was sensible enough to

know that she had better go back to Napoleon at once. Because of a guily conscience and the fear of losing her husband if she drove him too far, she threw herself into his arms and became the passionate, loving woman who had so completely infatuated him before they were married. Day and night they were absolutely inseperable.

A young artist who had been commissioned by the Government to paint the General's portrait was totally unable to get him to pose for it.

Whenever he managed to get his subject into the room of the palace which had been set aside for the work, Napoleon would spring up and call for his wife and they would start to make love before the embarrassed young man.

Finally, the only way he was able to get a rough likeness of Napoleon's face so that he could complete the formal picture of the General marching at the head of his troops, was at breakfast time, when Josephine drew Napoleon onto her lap, holding and fondling him like a mother with her child.

This period of complete reconciliation and the return to the amorous behaviour of their first few weeks of knowing one another was extremely brief. In this fickleness Josephine was regarded by those around her as extremely foolish. In actual fact she was unintentionally much cleverer than any other woman in Napoleon's life.

She had the sensitivity to realise that the whole of Napoleon's make-up was channelled to the prosecution of war. The only stimulus to his mind and heart was the resistance of others to his wishes. Such resistance always brought out his genius to the full and he concentrated all his power and determination on succeeding by guile, by force or by intelligence.

For most of the time that he was acquainted with or married to Josephine she see-sawed between periods of coldness alternating with bursts of passion the like of which he never experienced with any other woman.

These were his victories just as the long periods of coldness were examples of hostility which were a challenge he was unable to resist.

Josephine never let him know that she was a willing victim or that she had singled him out at the very onset of their acquaintance. Always she insinuated that he conquered her against her better judgement.

Always she reminded him that, pure and chaste, he had seduced her before they were legally married.

'No other man attracts me, or ever will,' she would reiterate. 'As you say so often, I am cold by nature.'

If Josephine had been a willing and devoted mistress and, after marriage, a placid and obedient wife, there can be little doubt that Napoleon's interest would have quickly waned.

As it was, he wrote to her on February 3rd, 1797, from Forli:

I idolise you, and send you a thousand kisses.

5

The capitulation of the Austrian army left Napoleon virtually conqueror of all Italy.

The final clearing up of pockets of resistance he left to his generals and he hastened back to the Serbolloni Palace in Milan, to be united with his wife.

He was slowly understanding how to keep Josephine happy even if he could not devise ways to retain her affection. One thing which delighted her was that her son, Eugène, was appointed an *aide-de-camp*. This meant he could live with them.

Napoleon's adoration of Josephine was known by all those close to him. Marmont, writing of the Italian campaign, said:

Bonaparte was continually thinking of his wife. He desired her and awaited her with impatience. . . . He often spoke to me of her and of his love with all the frankness, fire and illusion of a young man.

One morning at Tortona the glass in front of his wife's portrait, which he always carried with him, broke in his hands. He grew frightfully pale and suffered the keenest alarm.

'Marmont,' he said to me, 'my wife is either ill or unfaithful.'

Writing after their meeting at Milan, Marmont says:

Once in Milan General Bonaparte was very happy, for then he lived only for his wife; for a long time this had been the case; never did a purer, truer or more exclusive love fill a man's heart or the heart of so extraordinary a man.

As the summer heat made Milan too enervating the household was moved to Montebello, not far from Verona, where Napoleon commandeered a magnificent palace containing scores of rooms. The reason for this choice was not purely to please Josephine's love of the spectacular but to provide accommodation for the numerous members of the Bonaparte family whom he wished to entertain.

Rather surprisingly, Josephine went out of her way to placate Napoleon's mother—the suspicious Letizia Bonaparte. She was little more than a peasant but a woman of strong character. She had borne ten children but had kept both her figure and her health.

'You are killing yourself,' were Madame's first words to her son.

'On the contrary, I think I am very much alive,' Napoleon replied.

Josephine was nothing that Madame Bonaparte wanted in a daughter-in-law. She was older than Napoleon. She was not a Corsican. Her face was rouged. She had not come to her bridegroom a virgin, and had not merely previously been married but was known to have had several lovers. Napoleon had made her his wife without asking the formal permission of his mother.

All these difficulties Josephine overcame by doing everything she possibly could to placate the older woman. She treated her with more deference than she would show to the most distinquished aristocrat, and whenever Madame Letizia was present Josephine behaved with almost menial deference to her husband.

The result was that on the surface at any rate the two women got on quite well together. With the other members of the family, notably Napoleon's three sisters, things were not so happy. Joseph Bonaparte would have hesitated to relate to his mother the gossip about his brother's wife. But with his sisters he would have no such compunction.

Through this, or because of a natural jealousy for an outsider who had become a member of the family, there was

66

an implacable hatred between Josephine and the three young women.

Paulette was the prettiest creature you could see, wrote a friend at the time. *She had the behaviour of a schoolgirl, talking at random, laughing at everything and nothing, mimicking the most important personages, sticking out her tongue at her sister-in-law when she was not looking.*

The Bonaparte family all believed Josephine had been a familiar figure at the Court of Louis XVI. They thought her stuck up and a snob. They mistrusted her.

Josephine, on the other hand, thought the Bonapartes were coarse, ignorant peasants. Their faces unadorned by paint or powder were, she thought, what one could expect from low-caste Italians.

She was astonished to see how their presence made Napoleon wish to play boisterous games like a schoolboy. She also knew that behind her back his sisters spoke of her as a middle-aged widow with a shady past.

As a matter of fact, Napoleon's sisters were hardly any better morally than the women they thought fit to criticise. The youngest of the sisters, Paulette, a girl of seventeen, was at that time deeply involved in a scandal. She was having an affair with a forty-year-old man named Fréron, regional controller of Southern France, who did not seem to realise that the Reign of Terror had ended.

His ruthlessness might have made him acceptable as a good Republican but his political activities did not counteract the fact that his moral life was reprehensible even for those times. He boasted openly of the number of his illegitimate children scattered over the area which he ruled in the name of the Convention.

Napoleon was determined to end his sister's infatuation by marrying Paulette to one of his most brilliant generals, the twenty-four-year-old Victor Emmanuel Leclerc.

Because they were temperamentally somewhat alike and

were therefore able to see through each other's hypocrisy, Paulette and Josephine loathed one another. Paulette blithely agreed to the marriage arranged for her with Leclerc. Then, to her delight, she discovered that on her husband's staff was the young Hipployte Charles.

From the servants and possibly even from her husband, Paulette obtained every intriguing detail of Charles's adventures with Josephine. As soon as she had collected enough evidence she went to her brother and told him everything.

Napoleon was stunned. He had believed implicitly in Josephine's continual reference to the coldness of her nature, except where he was concerned. He had, with typical masculine conceit, really thought that he was the only man who could arouse her passion.

Over and over in his letters he had referred to her coldness, her chastity. He had proof of this and Josephine's protestations that other men's advances repulsed and revolted her were easy to believe.

Now at Paulette's revelations he was smitten to the heart. He had Hippolyte Charles arrested.

As soon as he had him behind bars, Napoleon reached around for an excuse to punish him without disclosing to the world the real reason for his detention. It was not difficult to discover formidable examples of bribery and corruption which had not only increased Charles's wealth but had deprived the army of much-needed supplies at a critical phase of the Italian campaign.

The charges were serious enough for Napoleon to have had Hippolyte Charles shot. For some days Napoleon did, indeed, sit brooding in his study refusing to see anyone, and trying to make up his mind to order his rival's execution.

Finally he decided that such a sentence on a man who had not actually shown cowardice or definite treachery on the field of battle and at a time when hostilities were over, would be both unjust and unwise. Napoleon therefore contented himself by dismissing Hippolyte Charles from the army.

Josephine had not been allowed to approach Napoleon

during this period of indecision. She was not only desperately upset at losing Hippolyte Charles but she was also frightened how Napoleon would act.

'My sister-in-law,' Paulette said subsequently to the Duchesse d'Abrantés, 'almost died of grief. And certainly one does not die of grief at parting from one's friends. There must have been more than friendship in this case. As for me, I consoled my brother, who was very unhappy.'

If Napoleon felt that this action against Hippolyte Charles had restored his marriage to a proper basis and had repaired the damaged reputation of his wife he was sadly wrong.

At the very time that Charles was being escorted from Italy back to France, news came of a carousal of some of his officers at which Murat had been the principal guest. The party had gone on until late at night and there had been much drinking. The main drink of the evening was a punch he had made himself. During the preparations he produced a curious silver-gilt utensil from a case.

'What's that?' one of his guests asked.

'It is used for squeezing the oranges and lemons I use in the punch when I make it Creole fashion. It is, in fact, a souvenir from my teacher in the art of punch making.'

After a great deal of punch and champagne the swarthy, handsome Murat began to brag of the beautiful Creole who had taught him not only how to make punch but many other delightful things.

Then one of his officers, taking the lemon squeezer in his hand, noticed there were two initials engraved on it.

That same evening Bonaparte heard about the party and sent a message to Murat requesting that the lemon squeezer which had been such a success should be sent to him. Unfortunately, no one could find it.

'It's a pity that it is lost,' Murat said to his friends, 'I thought so much of it that I had my initials engraved upon it. "J.M." for Joachim Murat.'

'But someone said it was marked "J.B.",' one protested.

'What nonsense!' Murat cried. 'We had all drunk too

much and in that condition is is easy to mistake M for B.'

Bonaparte was known to take a dislike to Murat from that day. When he drew up a list of officers to accompany him to Egypt, Murat's name was not among them.

To his annoyance, however, and great surprise, Murat was appointed by the Minister of War to take command of a regiment of Dragoons.

'Who has got Murat this appointment?' he asked.

No one was brave enough to tell him that Madame Bonaparte was responsible. She liked Murat and still had a great deal of influence with Director Barras.

As usual Josephine saw the danger signs and set out to make herself irresistible to her husband. The Bonaparte family returned home and Napoleon and Josephine were left to themselves.

Day after day there were parties and receptions for representatives from the towns and principalities of the conquered countries bringing gifts and tokens of esteem. Napoleon basked in all this ostentatious veneration of his importance and was greatly impressed by the manner in which the delegations paid their respects to his wife.

For herself, Josephine found the situation delightful. The treasures of Italy which were showered upon her appealed to her Midas-like greed for collecting anything and everything.

Despite the nagging question of Josephine's infidelity Napoleon found this period the happiest of all with his wife. He looked remarkably healthy and well and he was boisterously full of good humour.

Throughout his life he searched for symbols of good fortune which might perhaps in themselves be of a minor character but which were important as indicating a change.

One such stroke of luck which he humorously but sincerely cited as proof that all was at last going well was the death of Fortuné. The quarrelsome little dog who had intimidated everyone from Napoleon downwards with his snappiness and his constant yapping, met his match in the garden of the Palace at Montebello when a mongrel resented Fortuné's barking, launched himself upon him and ripped his throat out.

'You can imagine the grief of poor Fortuné's mistress,' Napoleon said to his *aide-de-camp*. 'I did, of course, show my sympathy but I could not forget that his death has left me full possessor of my wife's bed.'

Napoleon's triumph was short-lived. Within a week a small puppy, the exact breed and colour of the lamented Fortuné the First, was lying growling on the bed.

The mongrel belonged to the head chef. One evening some weeks later, Napoleon saw the chef taking the air some distance from the Castle. As soon as he saw his master he rushed into some bushes and tried to hide.

Bonaparte walked up to him.

'Why do you run away from me?' he asked.

'General, after what my dog did . . .'

'Well, what about it?'

'I was afraid you would not like to see me.'

'Where is your dog? Haven't you got him any longer?'

'Forgive me, General, but I do not allow him to set so much as a paw in the garden now that Madame has got another dog.'

'Let him come as often as he likes,' Napoleon commanded. 'Perhaps he will rid me of the other brute!'

At the end of the summer Napoleon made a triumphant return to Paris while Josephine followd more slowly. Napoleon was fêted night after night and he became bored whereas Josephine was beside herself with happiness, not only because of the adulation which was shown to her but also on account of a renewal of her friendship with Barras.

Though Napoleon was evidently ready to accept this situation there was another defect of his wife's which was rankling more and more.

At a party given by Talleyrand at the Hotel Gallifet to which four thousand guests were invited with Napoleon and Josephine as the guests of honour, he appearing in modest civilian clothes while Josephine selected one of her Greek goddess costumes, Napoleon was waylaid by Madame de

Staël, the notorious and talented woman of Parisian society who let it be known that she had written to Napoleon offering herself to him.

Madame de Staël contrived to get Napoleon alone whilst Josephine was talking to Barras. As she was regarded as one of the most brilliant conversationalists in the capital, she soon had a crowd around her on tenterhooks to know what she would say to the General. She made the best of her opportunity.

'General,' she asked, 'who is the woman you love most?'

'My wife,' Napoleon replied.

'Of course,' said Madame de Staël, 'but which is the one you would regard most highly?'

'The one who best knows how to look after her home and family.'

'Yes, General. I understand and agree,' said Madame de Staël, 'but which woman would be in your opinion the first among all women?'

Napoleon did not answer for a time, standing in his characteristic way with his head slightly bent, pondering and sifting in his mind for the right answer. Finally he said:

'The one who bears the most children.'

Madame de Staël smiled.

'You are a wise man, General.'

The remark was a minor triumph for Madame de Staël. The guests who had heard the exchange took good care that the story of Napoleon's hope for children was spread far and wide.

Josephine was hurt more than angry when the story came to her ears. She knew that her inability to conceive was a matter of deep unhappiness to Napoleon. What made it worse was that she had already borne at least two children.

No man likes an aspersion on his masculinity, least of all a belligerent man like Napoleon, accustomed to get what he wanted and to prove that physically and mentally he was superior to every man around him.

Although at this time Napoleon was a long way from becoming Head of State, there can be little doubt that dreams of founding a dynasty were constantly in his mind, and the problem of providing an heir must have been an important one to him.

Apart from this, his Corsican peasant background meant that in the eyes of his family he was failing his destiny in being married but in not being a father.

The ceaseless round of futile gaiety in Paris, the occasionally unwise behaviour of his wife in the presence of others, and the still serious international situation drove Napoleon from the capital.

His generals had been far busier than he, massing and training armies in Northern France in readiness for the invasion of England. At Wimereux, not far from Boulogne, a vast harbour was being constructed to protect the large number of barges which had been commandeered from the rivers and the coastal waters of France.

In Paris they gossiped at the parties that the success of invasion was a foregone conclusion. Napoleon was too good a general to take the optimistic view of the politicians and the social butterflies of the capital. He knew more about strategy than his enthusiastic young officers in the Channel ports who blithely told him that all was ready.

In fact, after a short tour from Dunkirk to Boulogne early in February, 1798, Napoleon took the view that the enormous preparations that had been made were futile. The invasion of England was impossible.

As soon as he had made this decision, Napoleon's agile mind turned to other fields of conquest. His vision ranged to the east where the vast wealth of England in India could be the ultimate goal.

Having come to the decision that Egypt should be the next arena for conquest, Napoleon hurried back to Paris, much to Josephine's annoyance and temporary alarm.

While her husband had been away Josephine had been constantly visiting the Luxembourg Palace at night to be with Barras.

Napoleon returned unexpectedly, and with deliberate secrecy so that the English spies should not glean the knowledge that preparations to resist invasion along the Kent and Sussex coast could safely be relaxed.

Josephine was preparing to visit Barras when she heard a noise in the hall below her boudoir and guessed that Napoleon had returned.

Quickly she wrote a note and sent it by a discreet manservant to Barras's secretary.

Bonaparte arrived tonight. Please, my dear Botot, express my regrets to Barras that I shall not be able to dine with him. Tell him not to forget me. You know better than anyone how I am placed. Au revoir. My sincere friendship.

6

Preparations for the Egyptian expedition took close on three months, during which time Napoleon was naturally preoccupied with military matters. So, for that matter, was Barras who, as Director, had to share with Napoleon the enormous amount of organisation involved.

This meant that Josephine was left largely to her own devices and she seems to have occupied her time mainly with her children.

Finally, on May 3rd, it was time for Napoleon to start on his long journey. Josephine accompanied him as far as Toulon where he was to embark with the fleet of troop transports and ships of the line.

She walked with him on to the jetty. He clasped her in his arms, descended a step, returned and held her close.

'God knows!' he exclaimed, 'how long it will be!'

Josephine was crying bitterly. They mingled tears and kisses.

When he started out Napoleon had conceived the idea of taking Josephine to Egypt with him, partly because he could not face the thought of being by himself for what would undoubtedly be a long period, but also to avoid any unfortunate occurrences of infidelity as had happened in Italy.

Josephine was not enamoured with the idea and pleaded ill-health. Napoleon, who always liked to regard women as naturally delicate, accepted her statement and the discussion developed into a question as to whether her lack of good health was one reason for her infertility. The upshot was that he advised her to take a couple of months' rest so that she could undergo a course of treatment at the spa of Plombières, a well-known resort in the foothills of the Vosges Mountains.

After a course of treatment there she was to come to Egypt, by which time the worst of the heat of the summer would be over.

Josephine had little desire to accede to the last part of her husband's request and Fate, rather fortunately, helped her to get out of it. Soon after she commenced taking the waters at Plombières she was standing with some friends on a rickety balcony outside her bedroom admiring the view, when the structure collapsed, hurling her to the ground but breaking no bones.

Josephine, however, regarded this accident as a good enough reason to play the invalid for nearly three months, until, with the first chill of autumn, she returned to Paris.

This return to the capital had been approved by Napoleon after he had received news of his wife's accident. He hoped that after a further rest she would set out for Egypt, travelling at a leisurely pace as far as Naples and then taking ship from there.

Once again Fate came to Josephine's aid. After the victory of Nelson at the battle of Aboukir Bay, there was really no possibility of any French ship reaching Egypt without being chased and, very possibly, captured by the enemy.

Josephine decided to make the best of her separation from her husband by setting up her own household. She was really very pleased with the situation. Her husband was far away and yet she still had all the kudos and glory of being his wife. Napoleon had put all his personal fortune, which by this time was quite considerable, in the hands of his brother with the instructions that from it he should pay Josephine 4,000 francs a month for her personal expenditure.

This was not a very large sum, but with all her household expenses taken care of, the allowance was, in fact, merely pocket money and she should have been able to manage easily.

She launched on a period of great extravagance. One of the first things she did was to complete the purchase of Malmaison, near the village of Rueil, which she had seen during

76

the early months of her marriage and which she had tried to persuade Napoleon to buy.

He also thought the house a good one and was prepared to pay a quarter of a million francs for it. The deal was not completed when he left for Egypt and Josephine, without obtaining her husband's approval, signed the deeds of purchase. So far from trying to get a better price than her husband had tentatively offered, she offered another 40,000 francs for the furniture.

She had not anything approaching the sum required. All she could do was to pay cash for the furniture and fittings and to use her monthly allowance to pay the interest on the debt. This amounted to just over 200,000 francs.

Josephine rushed into this purchase without taking adequate advice and only after the deal was completed was it realised that the place was in an appalling condition. What really appealed to her was its vast size, which made it a sort of rural palace, and she liked even more the large grounds in which it stood.

To Malmaison she brought all her accumulated treasures. She hung the walls with the superb collection of old masters which had been given her by the Pope and various Italian cities. She had the marble statues from Austria placed in the corridors and in the parks. Her salons were adorned with Florentine mosaics and she needed coffers, boxes, chests and cupboards to accommodate her wonderful pearls, diamonds and cameos.

For the rest of that summer and for the early part of the autumn she spent all of her time sorting out this jumble of beautiful and valuable *objets d'art*.

Unfortunately the house was most inadequately provided with the less spectacular but far more necessary pieces of equipment such as bedclothes, lights and kitchen utensils.

Josephine had hardly enough money when winter came to provide adequate heating. The great barn of a place was full of draughts from cracked windows and ill-fitting doors and so subject to damp that mould formed on the walls.

Feeling it was too much for her to cope with she returned to

77

Paris and resumed her *liaison* with Barras. But even the Director had to stand aside when Hippolyte Charles turned up once again. Disgraced and dismissed from the army, he was one of the few men whom Josephine had met through her husband who was not either busily engaged in the Mediterranean ports or actually out in Egypt.

Hippolyte Charles was an opportunist, and if Napoleon had expected to ruin him he had misjudged his man. As he was no longer able to purchase materials for the French army he now set up as a contractor selling war supplies. He became extremely rich from this activity, his experience at the receiving end naturally making it easy for him to extract the last sou of profit from his deals.

As soon as spring made Malmaison habitable once more, Josephine returned there and Hippolyte Charles was a constant visitor, the local people believing him to be Josephine's son, so constantly was he staying in the house overnight.

The *liaison* became so scandalous that even Josephine's friends began to cut her. Patriotic Frenchmen and Frenchwomen were disturbed that the wife of their beloved General, at the time fighting for his life in Egypt, should behave in such a way and so blatantly traduce his honour. Some felt it their duty to inform Napoleon of what was going on.

Many letters bound for Egypt fell into the hands of the English, but some got through. Napoleon, on his way to the siege of Acre, was told what was happening at home.

Bourrienne recounts:

I saw Bonaparte walking alone with Junot, as was his custom. I was not very far away from them and I know not what made me watch him during their conversation. The General's face, which was always pale for some unknown reason, suddenly became still paler. The muscles of his face seemed to contract; his eyes became fixed and he struck his forehead several times. After about a quarter of an hour he left Junot and returned to me. I had never seen him look so angry or so preoccupied. I advanced to meet him; as soon as we were together he said in a harsh,

78

brusque tone: 'You are not my friend. Oh, women, women, Josephine! . . . If you really were my friend, you would have told me what I have just learned from Junot, he is a true friend. . . . Josephine! And we are parted by six hundred leagues! You ought to have told me. Josephine! To think that she should deceive me so. . . . She! . . . Woe betide them! . . . I will exterminate that breed of effeminate puppies and coxcombs! . . . As for her, I will divorce her. Yes, a divorce. And everybody shall hear of it. It is your fault. You ought to have told me.'

Bourrienne tried to pacify Napoleon, telling him of his great fame as the conqueror of Egypt.

'My fame?' Bonaparte cried. 'Ah, what would I not give to learn that what Junot has just told me was not true! So dearly do I love that woman. If Josephine is guilty, a divorce shall separate us for ever. I won't be the laughing stock of all the good-for-nothing devils in Paris. I will write to Joseph, he shall get us divorced.'

Josephine had no intuition of what was happening in Egypt. She was madly happy with Hippolyte Charles. He was witty, amusing and handsome despite the fact that he was so small.

Gohier, the President of the Directory, brought her to her senses. She was invited to the Luxembourg and told she was creating a scandal.

'But Hippolyte and I are just good friends,' she protested. Gohier snorted.

'You tell me,' he said, 'that you and Citizen Charles are nothing more than friends. But as this friendship is so exclusive that it makes you forget the laws of decency and morality, I feel I must talk to you as if it were really a case of love and urge you to get a divorce. A friendship which can make you forget everything else will compensate you for what you will lose by divorce.'

Josephine realised that she had gone too far. She was well

aware that Hippolyte was only a playboy and that he would have little use for her if she were no longer Bonaparte's wife. She decided to rebut the gossip about her ceaseless intimacies with Hippolyte Charles by resuming her attachment to Barras.

In October, 1799, without any warning because of the lack of communications from Egypt in the face of the English naval blockade of the Mediterranean, news came that Napoleon had unexpectedly landed on the coast of Provence.

All his fellow officers with the armies in Egypt whose rank permitted a degree of intimacy, knew that Napoleon was determined to divorce his wife. He had actually requested one of his generals who was returning to France to select a house for him where he could live by himself.

I have a great deal of domestic trouble, he wrote, *for the veil is entirely rent. Arrange for me to have a country house ready to receive me, either near Paris or in Burgundy, on my arrival in France. I mean to pass the winter in the country and to live the life of a hermit. I am sick of my fellow creatures. I am in need of solitude and isolation, and earthly splendours weary me. My heart is worked out with suffering. Glory is but a poor thing at twenty-nine years of age. I have drained the cup of human bliss: I now only have to become a thoroughly selfish creature. I mean to keep my house to myself: I will share it with nobody. I no longer have anybody to live for.*

Adieu, my only friend. . . .

Miserably Napoleon even tried to restore his sense of self-respect by playing tit-for-tat. He started a rather tawdry affair with the attractive, witty wife of an infantry lieutenant. She was a Madame Fourés, one of the few Frenchwomen who had managed to reach Egypt to be with her husband.

Napoleon made this affair as ostentatious as possible. He rented a house for his mistress adjoining the palace in Cairo where he himself had set up his headquarters, and found a pretext to send the woman's husband home.

Unfortunately the ship on which Lieutenant Fourés sailed was captured by the English. As they knew from their spies what his wife meant to Napoleon, instead of keeping him prisoner, they mischievously landed the poor man back in Egypt and gave him safe conduct to Cairo.

On October 13th, 1799, Josephine was dining with Director Gohier and his wife when she was handed a letter from Eugène. She opened it incredulously. It told her that he had landed in France with his stepfather. Napoleon was back. She turned deadly pale and the letter shook in her nervous hand.

'I must go and meet him!' she said.

At last she saw the danger she was in. The Bonapartes, with their hatred boiling up against her, would be waiting to tell Napoleon all the scandal of Paris. She knew she must go to him before they had time to harm her irrevocably.

'If only I am the first to see him he will throw himself into my arms,' she confided to a close woman friend.

There were two main routes between the South of France and Paris, both of them passing through Lyon, but northwards from there taking quite different routes.

Unfortunately Josephine chose the route through Burgundy and, finding the road deserted, she fondly believed that Napoleon was resting in Lyon.

On her arrival there, to her consternation , she learned that her husband, hailed everywhere as the Saviour of France, had gone the other way. Even now he must be approaching Paris. Without resting she turned round and went back. Travelling at a break-neck speed she arrived two days after Napoleon had reached Paris. He was told all that had been going on, the most damaging stories coming from his brothers who had been closely and gleefully watching Josephine's behaviour.

Napoleon made what he insisted was his final and irrevocable decision then and there. His married life was over. He would get a divorce. The Bonaparte family was delighted.

His friends, however, were worried. Citizen Collot, a sensible, level-headed man, came to breakfast with him. Napoleon unburdened his heart. Collot looked grave.

'Think of France,' he said. 'The eye of the nation is fixed on you. France expects you to devote your life to her well-being; if she sees that you allow yourself to be worried by domestic quarrels your glory will fade. She will look on you as one of those luckless husbands whom Molière was so fond of holding up to ridicule. Leave you wife and her faults alone.'

'No! I have made up my mind,' Napoleon answered. 'She shall not set foot in my house any more. What do I care for what people will say? They will cackle for a day or two and then, on the third day, they will forget all about it. The future is so big with events; what effect will our separation have? It will have no effect whatever on me. My wife shall go to Malmaison. I shall stay here. The public knows quite enough about the matter not to be mistaken as to my reasons for sending her away.'

Collot argued for some time. When he was leaving he said:

'Your violence proves to me that you are still very much in love with your wife. When she appears and begs to be forgiven you will forgive her and you will feel happier.'

Napoleon was furious.

'I forgive her?' he shouted. 'Never! You know me well enough. If I were not sure of myself, I would pluck my heart out of my body and throw it into the fire.'

Late that night, after his friends and relatives had left him, Napoleon locked himself up in his study in the house on the Rue de la Victoire and brooded on the disaster that had come to his personal life.

He heard the noise of horses' hoofs and a carriage on the cobble-stones outside and the sound of running footsteps and doors opening and shutting. Josephine had arrived after her non-stop journey from Lyon, tired, dishevelled and crying.

He moved to the door and reassured himself that it was locked and bolted just as Josephine started to knock on it and call his name over and over again.

'Open the door, *mon ami, mon bon ami*. I will explain everything!'

She cried out that she loved him. She then lapsed into incoherence, finally wailing at the top of her voice.

Still Napoleon refused to open the door. Beside herself with exhaustion and fear, Josephine lay down on the floor weeping bitterly, knocking the door with her feet and bumping it with her head.

At last she saw the pit into which she had fallen—saw Malmaison unpaid for, the debts accumulating around her, the loneliness when people were no longer interested in her, old age creeping towards her!

She passed a terrible night of utter misery and humiliation, and when the morning came she began to prepare for her departure. It was then she had an idea. She roused Hortense and Eugène and told them what they must do.

They sent a humble request to Napoleon that they might say 'good-bye' to him before they left his house. Napoleon agreed immediately. His brother Joseph was with him in his study when he received his stepchildren. Falling on their knees, they blurted out what Josephine had told them to say.

'Don't desert our mother—it would kill her.'

Napoleon, looking wretchedly ill and unhappy, said in a low voice:

'Very well. Go and fetch your mother.'

Josephine was lying bent with grief on the stairs leading to the servants' quarters. She looked old and broken. She was not pretending or acting a part—she was at the end of her tether.

'Mama, come!' Hortense cried. 'The General is waiting for you.'

Eugène led Josephine to Napoleon's room. She was weeping so bitterly she could hardly see him, but stretched out her hands and fell to the floor in a faint. Napoleon caught her in his arms and laid her on the sofa.

When she opened her eyes only Joseph was in the room with Napoleon. She gave a little cry as she saw the stern coldness of her husband's face.

Napoleon asked her if it was true what he had been told

about her relationship with Hippolyte Charles. Josephine was past lying.

'Yes, it is true,' she said.

Napoleon instantly flew into a rage. It was obvious that he had expected her to deny it. He told her to leave the room immediately and go to Malmaison.

Broken beyond defiance and past even pleading for herself Josephine rose unsteadily to her feet and went from the study.

Napoleon said afterwards to Collot:

'I never saw anything like it in my whole life. And there was that great booby, Joseph, listening the whole time. . . . As she was coming downstairs, crying, I saw Eugène and Hortense following her, sobbing. God did not give me a heart to let me see tears shed without feeling moved myself. . . . Eugène was with me in Egypt. I have accustomed myself to look on him as my adopted son; he is so brave; he is such a good boy. Hortense is just coming out; all who know her speak highly of her. I confess I was deeply moved. I couldn't resist the sobs of those two poor children. I said to myself: "Are they to be the victims of their mother's ill-conduct?" I stopped Eugène. Hortense turned back with her mother. I said nothing. How could I help it? Every man is weak.'

When Lucien called at midday to talk about the divorce, he found Napoleon and Josephine in bed together.

7

Once again Josephine had extricated herself from an awkward situation. This time she had not attempted to lie to Napoleon by denying infidelity. But she had, by fervid statements of her adoration for him, convinced him that of all the men in her life, he was the only one who really mattered. With this he was apparently content.

Napoleon stipulated that she should never see Hippolyte Charles again, and she never did. But his hatred of the 'little lady's man' remained.

One day a long time later Napoleon, then the Emperor, was walking arm-in-arm with Duroc to see the Austerlitz Bridge which was then in the course of construction. A cab passed them in the street. Duroc felt the hand on his arm tighten and grow suddenly heavy.

He turned and saw that Napoleon was very pale.

'What is wrong?' he asked, thinking that the Emperor was about to faint.

'Nothing,' Napoleon replied peremptorily, 'be quiet!'

The occupant of the cab was Hippolyte Charles.

The only bitter remark Napoleon made was to Réal. 'The warriors from Egypt are like those from the siege of Troy,' he said, 'and their wives have been equally faithful!'

As soon as Napoleon's relatives could get him alone, they gave him vivid descriptions, both true and untrue, of Josephine's reprehensible behaviour in the past months.

Napoleon was probably prepared to take much of this with a grain of salt. He knew that his sisters and brothers were jealous of Josephine, but he was disturbed to find that his mother, who had seemed to like her daughter-in-law, was as critical as her children.

The reason was that Josephine, so open-minded that she could never resort to such hypocrisies as pretending to love her mother-in-law, had completely neglected the old lady. She had neither written to her nor called to see her when Madame Bonaparte came to live in Paris.

It was a serious failure on her part in the long war between Josephine and the Bonaparte family. Nine years later Josephine was to have good reason to regret that she had not consolidated her early friendship with 'Madame Mère' as she could easily have done.

Meantime Napoleon was prepared to forgive his wife's infidelities for two good reasons. One was that he knew he could not bear to live apart from Josephine. There had been reasons enough why he should do so, and his common sense told him that demands of honour and self-respect insisted that he should. But it was useless! Life without knowing that Josephine was his was a hell of frustration and suspicion.

The second reason was that he needed Josephine socially. The man who was later to emulate and even outclass the rigid, stilted ritual of Royal France was still acutely sensitive to his lack of breeding.

Still under thirty, Napoleon found that his military power and his popularity with the common folk were insufficient to override the social graces of the people with political influence. He was, of course, quite wrong in ascribing breeding and leadership to these people. Most of them were of as lowly origin as he and had attained power by far less commendable means.

But Napoleon could not see this; he was completely bemused by the aura of wealth, power and pomp which disguised the tawdry actuality.

He was impressed by the fact that Josephine's guardian and father-in-law was a Marquis and that her dead husband had been within the inner circle of the French Court. He envied her for having friends among the members of the aristocracy who had survived the Terror.

In his anxiety to find some link between himself and this

so-called glory of eternal France he completely overlooked the fact that Josephine was the daughter of an impoverished Colonial, that her dead husband had taken his title without real justification.

Napoleon never stopped to ponder on the fact that every real aristocrat had gone to the guillotine or had fled the country. He didn't realise that his wife's titled friends had been mere nonentities during the Royalist regime.

All he could see was that Josephine was the obvious bridge between a humble Corsican and the exalted nobility.

His desire for a go-between was not solely on account of snobbery but to weaken the power of the Republicans. His ambition now was not merely to lead the armies of France to victories which would bring the whole world under the tricolour. He wanted to enjoy the political fruits of these martial triumphs for himself.

Napoleon, in fact, had determined to become a Dictator. Three weeks from the day he set foot on French soil at Frejus in Provence—that port which significantly had seen Julius Caesar set out on his conquest of Gaul, Britain and eventually to preside over the Roman Empire—Napoleon had destroyed the Directory and had become First Consul.

It was a fantastic triumph. History has not paid sufficient attention to Josephine's contribution, so bemused have the historians been with the abilities of Napoleon.

He was, of course, of rare ability but he could not have taken the series of actions he did without the information which Josephine provided.

Her social influence, which is what Napoleon thought would be most useful to him, was greatly overrated. Josephine had little power to influence men and women of social and political importance. Her only chance was when men felt sufficiently attracted to start an *affaire* with her. Such incidents were obviously limited in number, and the men who found Josephine appealing were not the few and ageing pro-Royalists.

But of the activities of men like Barras and his colleagues in the Directory she had enormous knowledge. It must be remembered that Barras had time and time again employed her as the official hostess at his dinners and parties. The gatherings ranged from half a dozen politicians at a discreet dinner party to many hundreds of the élite of Paris at some celebratory ball.

At all these functions Josephine had rarely been far from the side of Barras and had listened to all his intrigues and political moves. What was more, like many men before him, he talked to his mistress. The significance of what she heard was doubtless lost on her, but she had a photographic memory so that she could repeat to Napoleon precisely what had been said.

Even Hippolyte Charles had been useful. He knew of every corrupt and venal official in the political world. These weak characters were remembered by Josephine and the nature of their weaknesses were now described to her husband.

Napoleon glowed with admiration for his wife's perspicacity. She, rather surprised that all the gossipy tittle-tattle she recounted was evidently so important, resourcefully took the opportunity to consolidate her own position.

'The circumstances attending my marriage with Madame de Beauharnais,' Napoleon said, 'put me in touch with a party whose aid was absolutely necessary to me if I wanted to carry out my scheme of coalition, one of the strongest points in my system of Government and one of its chief characteristics. Without my wife's help I could never have had any friendly intercourse with this party.'

The poet Arnhault, who was one of the habitués of Josephine's salon, wrote a vivid account which reads:

The rooms are full. Josephine does the honours of her salon more gracefully than ever. We meet men holding all sorts of opinions, generals, deputies, royalists, Jacobins, abbés, a Minister and even the president of the Directory. To see the air of superiority of the master of the house, one would think that he was already a monarch surrounded by his court. Here comes the Minister Fouché: he takes a seat on the sofa beside Mme Bonaparte.

Gohier: 'Anything new, citoyen Minister?'
Fouché: 'New? Nothing indeed.'
Gohier: 'Well?'
Fouché: 'Always the same tittle-tattle.'
Gohier: 'What do you mean?'
Fouché: 'They can talk of nothing but the conspiracy.'
Gohier (shrugging his shoulders): 'What conspiracy?'
Fouché: 'Why, the conspiracy. But I'm not so easily taken in as all that! I can see pretty straight, citoyen Director. Trust in me: they won't catch me napping. If a conspiracy really existed—since they will talk of such things—should we not see signs of it on the place de la Revolution or on the plaine de Grenelle?'

So saying, Fouché bursts out laughing.

Mme Bonaparte: 'Fie, for shame, citoyen Fouché! How can you laugh at such things?'
Gohier: 'The Minister knows what he's talking about. Don't be alarmed, citoyenne: if he thought that such a conspiracy really existed, he would be the last person to talk about it in the presence of ladies. Do as the government does: Don't let these rumours worry you. Sleep calmly!'
Bonaparte listens with a smile on his face.

The *coup d'état* began on November 9th, 1799, and was complete by the evening of November 10th.

Josephine stayed in the house in the Rue de la Victoire. Most of the time she was in bed in the room covered with mirrors where she had spent her wedding night. Despite the anxieties of conspiracy, Napoleon managed to return to the house in the early hours of the 10th. Josephine was wide awake. He lay down and told her of all the trials and near disasters of the day, ending, as he took her in his arms, with the news that he had triumphed! After a few hours' sleep he awoke and went to the Luxembourg, the master of France.

Josephine was now a queen in all but name. Within twenty-four hours she and and Napoleon had removed to the Luxembourg, staffed with the same servants she had known when Barras ruled there.

Now their previous contempt for a woman they knew was their master's mistress changed to humility and deference. For the first time since the Revolution had ordered the abolition of all civil titles except for Citizen and Citizeness, Josephine was, by Napoleon's express order, addressed as 'Madame.'

Some of the men who had assisted Napoleon in the overthrow of the government were disturbed by this and similar signs of undemocratic behaviour. They were not yet prepared to accept the reality that France was not under an oligarchy, but an autocracy.

For the time being Napoleon contented himself by restoring the old glory in social activities only. This meant, in effect, that he had to pursue the role of the simple soldier while his wife could act the grand-dame.

It was not difficult for her. She had a natural charm of manner and an open-hearted friendliness which disarmed those who came to criticise.

'Without being exactly pretty,' Madame Rémusat says, 'her whole person was wonderfully charming. Her features were refined and regular, her eyes had a gentle, soft expression.'

Where the new regime was concerned Josephine could hardly put a foot wrong, for she was, in fact, establishing a new social era instead of reviving the old one. Such items of etiquette as she knew about, or had heard from her aunt, were taken as evidence that the wife of the First Consul was an observer of the more polished ways of the past. If, in her exuberance—and Josephine was the type of person who absorbed vitality from friendliness and good fellowship—she did something rather novel or even shocking, well, she was merely setting the standard for the new society.

The only social sin she could have committed at this time would have been to be sullen, cold and unfriendly. This she could never be.

Josephine's qualities as a hostess were a strong contrast to the defects of Napoleon as a host. By temperament he was taciturn except when outlining future campaigns or describing past ones. And indigestion often made him ill-tempered after dinner. Moreover, anxious as he was to establish himself as arbiter of social taste, he could not help becoming impatient at the trivialities which were seemingly the only conversation among the ex-aristocrats, political turncoats and civil personages who flocked to his house.

Napoleon watched his wife with a mixture of envy, admiration and suspicion. The last because he did not intend to be embarrassed by a new rival for his wife's favours. He also took good care that every lady showed decorum, particularly when the hour was getting late and the gentlemen had drunk enough to risk a little boldness in their advances.

Then he would stride across the room and take Josephine by the arm.

'Come now, let's to bed,' he would say and lead her, without wishing their guests good night, towards their private suite.

The remark became famous throughout Paris.

Another story which delighted Parisians who suspected that a return to the excesses of the Court of the Bourbons was imminent was told of a party held shortly before Christmas. The night was frosty, and at first Napoleon's orders to the servants to make up the fires was regarded as the considerate action of a good host. But in the crowded rooms, with the logs blazing in stacks right up the chimneys, the place became stifling. Still Napoleon called for more fuel. Finally a servant dared to protest.

'There is no room for any more fuel, sir.'

Napoleon walked from fire to fire and nodded his satisfaction, conversation dying down as the guests wondered what was afoot.

'That will do for the time being,' he said. 'I want the fires to be kept burning fiercely, for it's an intensely cold night. Besides,' he added, pausing and glaring round the room, 'the ladies here are almost naked.'

The hint was not ignored. No more did Josephine wear a diaphanous gown or the more daring of her friends appear with their breasts almost completely exposed.

Proud of Josephine's success in welding the surviving aristocrats and the Republican leaders into a group entirely in favour of himself, Napoleon said to her:

'You will soon be living like a queen.'

When finally he persuded the Council of the Ancients to approve the removal of his official residence from the Luxembourg to the Tuileries, he rushed home in high spirits.

In his delight he pushed Josephine playfully, put his arms about her and threw her down on the bed. He felt as happy about the prestige of this residence for his wife as he did in the glory of it for himself.

Napoleon was discreet enough to remove most of the Royal insignia on the building and to have it named Government Palace to obviate any qualms that he was donning a regal mantle.

He also had the Third Consul and a number of ministers in the place in order to indicate that this magnificent home of Louis XVI was now a place of work as well as his own house.

The actual removal was made an excuse for a military parade. Josephine was sent on ahead so that she could watch from the windows of the Tuileries. Napoleon arrived in a coach drawn by six horses. He alighted to mount a charger in order to review his troops, who marched past with their battle honours and the tattered remnants of their flags which they had carried through Europe and a goodly part of the Middle East.

The sight of these evidences of Napoleon's devotion to France did much to allay murmurings about his Royalist trends.

Josephine had been assigned a suit of rooms on the ground floor, principally so that her bedroom could be the one which Marie Antoinette had used.

Napoleon took rooms on the first floor, which had been the private suite of the Kings of France. From his study-dressing room a staircase led from the interior of the wardrobe into Josephine's bedroom.

That night guests were encouraged to leave early, and when all was quiet Josephine tripped up the secret stairway to her husband's bedroom.

As she emerged from the wardrobe he turned to her and laughed aloud, strode across the room, gave her the affectionate smack on her behind which was his inevitable gesture of endearment.

'Come, little Creole,' he said. 'Come and sleep in the bed of your masters.'

8

Josephine gained less satisfaction from her new position than her husband. First came a change of the intimate manner of sleeping together.

'We lived like ordinary bourgeois folk in our private life,' Napoleon said, 'and we shared the same bed . . . but political events obliged me to change my customary ways for I found I had to work by night as well as by day.'

Part of their time was spent at the Castle of St. Cloud on the outskirts of Paris and Constant gives a striking picture of their love-life.

When first Napoleon came to live at St. Cloud, he always slept in his wife's bed. Later on, etiquette caused him to break this rule, and thus conjugal affection cooled somewhat. Indeed, the First Consul at last occupied apartments at some distance from those of Madame Bonaparte. In order to go to her, he had to walk down a long servants' passage, with rooms on either side occupied by members of the household, servants and others. When the First Consul intended to spend the night with his wife, he first of all undressed in his own rooms, and then went forth in a dressing gown and a handkerchief tied round his head. Torch in hand, I walked in front. At the end of the corridor there was a staircase, with fifteen or sixteen steps, leading to Madame Bonaparte's rooms. For her a visit from her husband was a great delight: everybody in the house was told about it next day. I seem to see her now, informing everyone she met, and rubbing her little hands as she said: 'I got up late this morning: but, you see, that's because Bonaparte came and spent the night with me!' On those days she was more than usually amiable, never refusing anybody anything, so that we always got just what we wanted. When the Empress spent the night in the Emperor's apartments, I entered the room as usual between seven and eight o'clock. I rarely found the illustrious pair asleep. The Emperor generally asked me for some tea, or orange-flower infusion, and got up at once. The Empress would say to him, smiling: 'What? are you going to get up? Lie still a little bit longer.' 'Well, you're not asleep, are you?' replied His Majesty; and then he would roll her in his counterpane, pat her cheeks and shoulders, and laughingly embrace her.

Another thing which upset Josephine about their new position was that Napoleon gradually but remorselessly got rid of all the men and women whom he considered to be of doubtful character or politically dangerous. Among these there happened to be the gay, frivolous and attractive people that Josephine counted as her friends.

She was utterly bored by the serious-minded civil servants and ex-officers of the army who were now taking over most of the departments of State on Napoleon's instructions. She was even more bored by their provincial wives.

She assuaged this boredom by indulging in tremendous extravagances particularly as regards jewellery. The purchases she made were far in excess of anything that Napoleon would permit or, indeed, afford. Deceiving her husband as regards financial matters worried Josephine no more than deceiving him by her infidelities had done.

Napoleon was surprisingly easy to mislead in these matters, in direct contrast to his piercing mind when political or military matters were under discussion. Partly to enhance the prestige and power of his family, but also to get rid of a past and still a potential future rival, Napoleon arranged the marriage of General Murat with his sister, Caroline.

Murat was not a wealthy man and he had to be encouraged to go through with the marriage by the expectation of a very handsome dowry from his bride. Napoleon arranged that the marriage settlement should include a gift of 30,000 francs from his own pocket and this left him with virtually no money at all to purchase a present for the bride.

From an unwilling Josephine he took a diamond collar for Caroline to wear at her wedding. The gift may have been worth, at the most, 10,000 francs. Josephine, to comfort herself for this loss, cast her eyes on a pearl necklace valued at half a million francs.

It was dangled in front of her greedy eyes by a fashionable Parisian jeweller named Foncier, who encouraged Josephine's avidity by saying that the pearls had once been worn by Marie Antoinette. Josephine knew that Napoleon would never countenance the purchase of such a costly article and she herself could not put her hands on a tenth part of the sum.

For days she walked about in a dream wondering how on earth she could get hold of the pearls. Her chance came when Berthier, Napoleon's War Minister, took her aside at a social function at the Tuileries and said:

'Your husband is a terrible Puritan these days. As you know, he insists that I must live at the Luxembourg so that I am continually at his disposal. At the same time he demands that my private life must be as perfect as my official one so far as the Luxembourg is concerned. This is indeed unfortunate because it is making someone besides myself miserable.'

Josephine was quick to understand what Berthier was trying to tell her.

'You mean that you and Madame Visconti cannot see as much of one another as you would wish?' she questioned.

Berthier smiled.

'You are, as I have always known, a woman of great understanding,' he murmured.

Madame Visconti was Berthier's latest mistress, a woman of great beauty and some notoriety. Napoleon had pointedly ordered his War Minister not to have the woman living at the Luxembourg or indeed even to allow her to visit him there.

Josephine was thoughtful for a few minutes and then she told Berthier about the pearls that Foncier had shown her, describing both their beauty and their history. Berthier immediately saw that she was offering him a deal, and said that if she would help him as regards his mistress, he believed that he could find her the money she needed for the pearls.

'During the coming weeks I expect to be allocated a considerable sum to pay for the hospital expenses of the army in Italy,' he said. 'The contractors have already made a vast fortune out of their supplies, and as regards the Italian landlords—after all, they are members of a conquered people and can be made to wait for their money.'

That night Josephine told Napoleon that Berthier and Madame Visconti were deeply in love with each other.

'Poor things,' she sighed. 'Fancy if you and I had been forbidden to see each other! How miserable we would have been!'

In a weak moment Napoleon agreed that so long as Berthier was discreet, he would raise no formal objection if he learned that Madame Visconti was living in his private quarters.

Next day Josephine sent a message to Berthier that all was well and he, in his turn, authorised her to use his name for credit with Foncier.

All was well now except that Josephine had no desire simply to gloat over the pearls in the privacy of her boudoir and she was too frightened to wear them. Napoleon was in the habit of looking at his wife before she attended any official function and criticising or commending her on her appearance. If she suddenly appeared with a magnificent necklace of pearls he would immediately notice it and demand to know where they had come from.

To extricate herself from this problem Josephine approached another of her many men friends, Napoleon's secretary, Bourrienne.

'I shall be wearing some new pearls,' she told him, 'at tomorrow's party. I won't put them on until after the party has commenced so that when Bonaparte notices them there will be plenty of people around. I would very much appreciate it if you would keep near me so that when I tell him that I have had them for a long time you will be able to support me.'

Bourrienne agreed to the plan. Sure enough, at the party on the following evening Napoleon stopped suddenly while talking to a group of his guests and strode across to his wife, saying:

'I have never seen those pearls before, have I?'

Josephine smiled.

'You must have noticed them, surely! These are the ones that the Cisalpine Republic presented me with when the delegate came to treat with you for peace. You must remember them, even though there were so many gifts at the time. Possibly you are misled because tonight I am wearing them round my neck whereas on previous occasions I have preferred to have them in my hair.'

Napoleon was still doubtful, so Josephine continued:

'You are getting like all husbands who never notice anything their wives wear! I'm sure Bourrienne has seen them before.'

She turned a questioning eye on Bourrienne who immediately obliged by saying:

'Yes General, I remember having seen them before.'

Bourrienne in his memoirs jesuitically:

After all, I was not lying for Madame Bonaparte had already shown them to me, and it was quite true that she had been given a pearl necklace by the Cisalpine Republic, but those pearls were incomparably less beautiful than these Foncier had produced.

Deceptions of this kind increased week by week. Josephine became very friendly with Fouché, Head of the Police. He was probably the most insidious, treacherous, and ruthless of all men in Napoleon's new administration.

Fouché had no compunction whatever of spying on his master with all the efficiency that he used to spy on Napoleon's enemies.

He told Josephine that it was essential for him to have all possible information about the people around Napoleon, even those the First Consul regarded as his friends and colleagues.

He added that it was Josephine's duty, as the leading woman of France, to supply him with all the information that she could, even though she herself might consider that sometimes it was breaking the confidence between husband and wife.

Josephine probably knew that this rigmarole was merely a front for Fouché's desire to consolidate his own position as the most powerful man in the Republic next to Napoleon.

While blithely agreeing to report regularly to the Head of the Police everything of interest that she heard either from friends of Napoleon, or from Napoleon himself, Josephine made it clear that she expected Fouché to pay for her services.

It was at first a modest sum, but so detailed and lavish were the items of information which Josephine provided for him at the delightful meetings they arranged secretly, that before long she was receiving more than 30,000 francs a month as an agent on the payroll of the French secret police.

The arrangement, as Fouché had always intended, put Josephine completely in his power. When the Head of Police decided that the Minister of the Interior, Lucien Bonaparte, was a potential danger he forced Josephine's help in getting rid of him.

Fouché may have been encouraged in this to some extent by patriotic motives. He knew that Lucien was trying to persuade Napoleon to set himself up as the first of a new hereditary line of rulers.

As Josephine had no child by Napoleon, Lucien thought that he himself might have a very good chance of inheriting the supreme position after Napoleon's death.

For a time Josephine and Fouché were the losers in this battle of wits, largely because Napoleon himself was, of course, in favour of Lucien's idea. In order to have a showdown Fouché finally used his powers of office to accuse Lucien Bonaparte of sedition against the Republic, and he insisted that he should be allowed to question the defendant in front of Napoleon.

Napoleon was alarmed at the situation. His brother had voiced the idea too quickly. The situation was extremely dangerous, for Fouché and his powerful allies might be able to bring the matter into the open and so cause his own downfall. He contented himself by saying that Lucien had merely been foolish but not treacherous.

Josephine had been listening outside the door to the raised voices of the three men and she decided that it was time that she intervened. Characteristically she did not rely on the strength of argument but on her own attractions.

In front of the cynically amused Fouché and the scowling Lucien, she walked across to Napoleon's desk, pulled his chair around and seated herself on his lap. She kissed him and running her fingers through his hair, said:

'I beg you, Bonaparte, not to make yourself king. It is that dreadful Lucien who is driving you to it. Don't listen to him.'

Josephine, as usual on these occasions, won the day. Lucien was dismissed from the Ministry of the Interior and put out of harm's way as Ambassador to Spain in Madrid.

It is not known what reward Fouché gave to Josephine for these special services but at any rate for the time being she had no worries about debts.

The question of successor to Napoleon was brought sharply in the people's minds in October 1800, when a plot to assassinate him misfired. It might also have disposed of Josephine.

Napoleon had announced that he intended to attend a performance of *The Creation* at the Opera in the company of Josephine and of various officials. It was also stated that he would travel in one carriage and Josephine in a second one. At the corner of a narrow street a cart, pulled by a decrepit old horse, moved very slowly across the road just as Napoleon's carriage approached, forcing the coachman to rein in his horses.

The coach would have had to stop completely if the mounted escort had not galloped on and whipped the cart-horse into activity, pulling the cart out of the way. Napoleon's carriage gathered speed. When it was a couple of yards past the cart there was a tremendous explosion. The cart, packed with gunpowder, blew up.

Apart from a shower of glass from the carriage windows which were sucked outwards, no harm was done to Napoleon's party, though there were more than thirty casualties among people standing in the street.

Josephine's carriage, which was quite a distance behind, also had its windows broken and Josephine's daughter, Hortense, who was travelling with her mother, was cut on the arm by a sliver of glass. Josephine fainted and slumped to the floor and for a moment it was thought she had been wounded. She was, however, unhurt.

Her enemies started the rumour that she knew that this attempt at assassination would take place. The insinuation was based solely on the fact that just before the party left the Tuileries she had some difficulty in fastening the clasp which held the shawl over her dress.

Napoleon's *aide-de-camp*, a man completely above suspicion, was largely responsible for the delay which occurred as he attempted to alter the pin so that the clasp worked. These few minutes did, however, mean that Josephine's carriage was some distance from that of Napoleon's at the time of the explosion.

If there had not been the delay Josephine's would have been only five or six yards behind her husband's. She would have received the full force of the explosion when Napoleon's carriage unexpectedly had a way cleared for it. Josephine and her companions would have been very seriously wounded if not killed.

Not even the greatest admirer of Josephine could say that she was a woman of undaunted courage. A risky plan which would inevitably take her within an ace of disaster even without a hitch to the arrangement would never have been acceptable to her.

Her faint was, on this occasion at any rate, perfectly genuine and she must have been terrified at the noise as the cart disintegrated.

Napoleon was not at all upset by the attempted assassination. When he arrived at the Opera House he said cheerfully:

'These rascals wanted to blow me up. Fetch me a book of the oratorio.'

Rumours had already reached the audience that the Saviour of France had been killed. Horrified, the whisper passed from person to person. Suddenly a thrill went through the crowded theatre—they raised their eyes to the Consular box.

Standing hand in hand with a pale, trembling Josephine was a slight figure, his eyes unclouded by fear. A great cry went up.

That night Paris gave Napoleon all her heart.

One result of this attempt on Napoleon's life was to bring home to him more forcibly than ever the problem of an heir. He was by now secretly determined that he would be the first of a dynasty of rulers of France. But, much as he loved his brother, he knew his plans would probably end in failure if, after his death, the succession had to go to a relative instead of to his own son.

It was because of this unshakeable conviction that he asked doctor after doctor to examine Josephine. He listened only to those who gave a favourable report of her potentiality to conceive and angrily dismissed any who pointed out that, at thirty-eight years of age and after six years of marriage, the likelihood of her bearing a child was remote.

No doctor could prescribe any drug or medicine that would help and Napoleon himself suggested that the allegedly magical properties of the waters of Plombières were the best hope, this despite the fact that Josephine had spent some time there while he was in Egypt.

Josephine agreed to visit the spa. While she remained in the family circle there was little chance of her forgetting her age and the ceaseless cry for an heir. One day the question of barrenness was raised and Josephine said hotly:

'You forget that I have already had children. Are not Eugène and Hortense mine?'

'But you were young then, my sister,' replied Elisa Bacciochi. Josephine burst into tears as Napoleon entered the room. He insisted on being told what had happened.

'How indiscreet of you,' he said angrily to Elisa. 'Do you not know that the truth is not always good to tell?'

Napoleon would talk in the most open way about the possibility of Josephine having a child. On one occasion when he discussed it in front of Lucien and several generals, he said that perhaps at her age it was unlikely.

Lucien took Josephine by the arm and remarked:

'Now, my sister, show the Consul he is mistaken and give us quickly a little Caesarion!'

From such embarrassing conversations Josephine escaped in the early summer of 1801 and went to Plombières. While there, she managed to surround herself with a number of amusing companions and Napoleon remained in Paris.

She went on to try the waters at Vichy but she was honest enough to admit to herself what she had known for a long time: that neither mineral waters nor magic potions could enable her to produce a child.

Her one consolation was that Napoleon still loved her. He wrote to her while she was away:

I love you as on the first day, because you are good and amiable above all things.

9

A less resourceful woman than Josephine might have lapsed into despair at the impossibility of her situation as regards an heir. But, as always in trouble, she was resourceful. Now she thought of what appeared to be a plan.

Her daughter, Hortense, was now a beautiful and attractive girl of eighteen. She had a slight, elegant figure, very lovely fair hair and large violet-blue eyes. She danced, drew, painted and sang, could play the piano and the harp and, later, composed music. Napoleon loved her.

'Hortense,' he said sometimes, 'compels me to believe in virtue.'

But as early marriages were the fashion it was high time that she was married. Louis Bonaparte was probably the most amenable and favourably inclined of his family towards Josephine. It was true that he had been ill and the sickness seemed to have affected his mind so that some of his activities bordered on eccentricity. What was more, his amorous activities were notorious throughout Paris, but he would, Josephine thought, in name at any rate, make an excellent son-in-law.

Things worked out admirably. Napoleon was agreeably pleased with the idea.

He had recently had a row with his brother Lucien and he was now prepared to adopt Louis as his favourite and his heir.

He said to an intimate friend:

'There is no further need to rack our brains to find a successor. I have found one—Louis. He has none of the faults of his brothers and he has all their good qualities.'

Louis was perfectly aware of the basic reason for the proposed marriage and was delighted to think that his child would inherit a dynasty without parallel in the world. Hortense, who had inherited both her mother's love of gaiety and a keen eye for the main chance, was perfectly content with the arrangement.

There was a great deal of criticism from outside people. The Duchesse d'Abrantés wrote later:

I do not claim that Josephine did not love Hortense. God preserve me from uttering such a thought! Still, I have my memories, and these memories bring me back words, facts and things which I do not believe compatible with a mother's love such as Hortense should have inspired.

Constant, who was Napoleon's valet, says that up to the very time of Louis's wedding he was having an *affaire* with a girl he had met casually in the Tuileries gardens, the daughter of an inspector of bridges.

Actually Louis, after his early promise in France and Italy, had suffered a great change in character. He had an illness in 1797 and there began a sentimental hypochondria, morose, jealous and vain.

Both Louis and Hortense had second thoughts on the eve of the wedding. Hortense suddenly discovered that she had fallen in love with one of her stepfather's *aides-de-camp*, a young man named Durot. For a time the passion between these two was so intense that Hortense told Napoleon that she could not go through with the proposed marriage.

Napoleon, a romanticist at heart, gently told her that if she really meant this, he would not stand in her way. But, because of the scandal which would be caused by an engaged girl carrying on a romance with someone else, she would have to go away from Paris and live in some provincial city where he would do his best to get her husband a decent military post.

Josephine was horrified at this last-minute hitch in the arrangements. On the evening before the wedding day matters came to a head when Durot sent his last love letter. In the final battle between the two women to see who would win, the letter lay on the table for hours. Eventually Hortense accepted defeat and sent it back to her lover unopened.

By this time, perhaps because he sensed she was in love with someone else, Louis had fallen in love with Hortense.

His brother Lucien hinted that there might be other reasons than the foundation of a dynasty to account for the anxiety of Josephine and Napoleon to get Hortense married.

Louis stammered that he was in love.

'You are in love,' Lucien records in his memoirs. 'Then why the devil do you ask my advice? Forget what I have told you. Marry her and God bless you.'

But the damage was already done. Lucien had repeated to his brother the story some vile scandal-mongers had invented —that Napoleon was in love with his stepdaughter.

Louis, morbidly suspicious by nature, did not forget and when he discovered an incompatibility of character with his wife he brooded over what Lucien had told him.

On January 4th, 1802, Louis Bonaparte and Hortense de Beauharnais were married. Josephine had gained her end.

'My daughter can only marry a prince or a Bonaparte,' she had said.

Josephine, who had little religious feeling, was very conscious of the fact that the civil marriages under the Republican regime were as easily undone as they were contracted. It was at her insistence that Hortense had a church ceremony as well as the civil one.

Napoleon, who also had very little religious belief, was steadily accepting the fact that due deference to the religious customs of the French people would be politically advantageous.

'The old fool of a Pope', to whom he had referred earlier when promising to turn France into a Protestant country, had now become a man whom Napoleon wished to placate.

In 1801 he had begun diplomatic talks to arrange a Concordat with the Vatican. After it had been signed in July of that year, Napoleon ordered that a solemn *Te Deum* should be chanted in the Notre Dame.

Some of Napoleon's Ministers, who were avowed atheists, tried to get out of taking part in the service, but Napoleon gave them definite orders that they should attend.

The impressiveness of the service, together with the knowledge that Napoleon was now committed to accept the dictates of the Roman Catholic Church as legally and morally binding, implanted in Josephine's worried mind still more strongly the fact that her own marriage, unblessed by any religious service, could easily be anulled.

'Bonaparte's real enemies,' she told Roederer, 'are those who put into his head ideas about a dynasty, about heredity, divorce and a second marriage.'

Rather pathetically she said on another occasion to one of the Councillors of State:

'Bonaparte listens to me with sufficient attention but his flatterers soon alter his opinions for him.'

This was the period of the very apex of Napoleon's triumphs. Wars were for the time being in abeyance. Napoleon had secured the left bank of the Rhine for France. The Austrian possessions in the Netherlands were his. The power of Venice had been stripped. Treaties completely favourable had been signed with Naples, Bavaria, Spain, Portugal, Russia, Turkey and Algiers. At Amiens an uneasy agreement had been signed with England.

But in May, 1803, war again broke out between England and France, and the occasion was taken by the power-intoxicated French nation as a reason for joyous celebration. They were convinced this was the eve of new triumphs that would make the French without question the only great power on earth.

For some weeks Napoleon made a tour of the whole country ending up on the Channel coast where the naval units and armies were preparing once again for the invasion of England.

Josephine accompanied him everywhere and she became immensely popular with all classes of people. She was still a most attractive woman. No one felt this to a greater extent than Napoleon, and there is the story of how he used to come to her room in the morning to see what she was going to wear that day, leading her before a mirror so that he might see her simultaneously on all sides at once.

'I shall be jealous of you when the public gazes at you today,' he said. 'Why are you so beautiful?'

His love for her coloured everything he did. One day when he was returning from a review and he was greeted by the crowds lining the streets with cheers and cries of affection, he said to Bourrienne, his secretary:

'Bourrienne, do you hear how their shouts of joy still re-echo! These sounds are as sweet to my ears as Josephine's voice; how happy and proud I am to be loved by such a nation.'

On the day before Napoleon was to be proclaimed Emperor of France he came to Josephine with the crown of diamonds and pearls she was to wear at the ceremony. It was worth more than a million francs. She let him place it on her head while tears of joy coursed down her cheeks, and caressed him in her usual way by making him sit on her lap.

Eight years earlier Napoleon had proposed to Josephine. One day when they were together, Josephine's lawyer, Raquideau, called and she went into another room to consult him. The door was left ajar and Napoleon heard the lawyer say:

'What! Marry a man with nothing but his sword and his uniform, who owns at most a little house! An unknown General, without a name, without a future, below all the great Generals of the Republic! Much better marry a shop-keeper!'

Napoleon pretended he had not heard but the evening before the Coronation, Raquideau was summoned to the Tuileries.

'I have sent for you,' Napoleon said to him, 'to give you a ticket for a front place in the Cathedral tomorrow so that you may be able to see clearly to what the unknown General has brought your client.'

The Coronation took place on December 2nd, 1804, at Notre Dame. The Pope annointed Napoleon who crowned himself, in order no one should think that he took his crown from the Church, as did the Holy Roman Emperors. Afterwards he crowned Josephine.

'At that moment,' said an eye-witness, 'he was really handsome and his countenance was lighted up with an expression of which no words can convey an idea.'

During the ceremony Napoleon whispered to Joseph:

'If our father could only see us now.'

Napoleon's wilful gesture in crowning himself and his Empress was intended to make the Pope 'unnecessary, only a simple witness and a supernumerary'. But the Holy Father, after a solemn prayer for the Emperor, said over the kneeling and crowned Josephine:

'May God crown you with the crown of fame and justice; may He arm you with strength and courage; so that by virtue of our blessing you may attain in true faith, because of the manifold fruits of your good deeds, the crown of eternal empire, by grace of the One whose power and kingdom last from eternity unto eternity.'

Josephine looked so lovely that everyone present spoke of her beauty. There was, however, an unfortunate incident after the actual crowning ceremony was completed. Napoleon and Josephine had to move away from the altar. Napoleon's sisters, who had naturally been most anxious to have prominent parts in the ceremony, had been ordered by their brother to be Josephine's train bearers.

Choking with rage they refused to dance attendance on the woman they hated.

'Very well,' Napoleon said, 'you will not be present at the Coronation.'

They gave in with a bad grace.

The train, of orange-red velvet embossed with golden bees and bordered and lined with ermine, was immensely long and heavy. It would have been quite impossible for anyone to walk unless the weight of it was taken by the bearers. When

Josephine rose from her kneeling position the two sisters deliberately refrained from lifting the train so that when she took a step forward she was pulled up abruptly and staggered, her foot knocking against the altar steps.

Napoleon's sisters openly showed their glee at this *contretemps* and it was only because Napoleon turned and spoke rapidly to them in a Corsican dialect that they sulkily picked up the train and the procession went on down the nave of the church.

The 'little Creole' from the West Indies was now Empress of all the French. She must, in that moment of triumph, have remembered the prophecy of the old native woman in Martinique.

Josephine's natural ebullience made her enjoy her new exalted position but there were a number of occasions when she was forced to think of the fantastic situation which was remorselessly and inevitably developing.

Napoleon was outdoing the Bourbons themselves in the grandiose nature of his life. Both he and Josephine had their own households and the occasions when she could get him alone became more and more rare. For the first time she knew what it was to feel jealous.

There had, of course, been stories of women when Napoleon was away on his military campaigns but for the most part they had merely been toys abducted for the amusement of the conqueror from the defeated nations. They had been chosen principally on account of their youth and beauty and with no rank of birth which made it even remotely feasible that Napoleon should promote them to the position of permanent mistress.

Now, however, from the Italian States with which he held treaties or which he had conquered, there had come a galaxy of beautiful women to the Coronation.

Napoleon was as nearly intoxicated with power as ever happened in his life. Even in the privacy of the Tuileries he strutted along like a potentate ogling and kissing any attractive woman he saw.

He particularly liked Josephine's readers, who by the nature of their duties were always within call of the Empress's private apartments. The result was that as fast as Napoleon appointed some pretty woman he had come across to the position of reader to the Empress, Josephine found an excuse to dismiss her.

Napoleon abandoned all discretion in these amours and Josephine, on entering her own boudoir one afternoon, found Napoleon kneeling at the feet of a pretty young girl who had the previous day been appointed reader.

The girl adroitly achieved some dignity by saying to the Empress:

'Please, your Majesty, remind your husband what he has apparently forgotten; that he is the Emperor whose duty it is to furnish to his people examples of virtue and wise behaviour.'

Josephine ordered her from the room and later got the War Minister to find a presentable young officer who could be told to marry the girl immediately on pain of dismissal from the army.

This shotgun wedding ceremony took place a day or two later. When Napoleon heard about it he was greatly angered.

'Very well,' he said. 'I shall send her husband so far from France that she will be glad to come and humble herself before me, to kneel at my feet as I at hers, begging me to cancel the appointment.'

Napoleon began to take a sadistic pleasure in paying back Josephine in her own coin. He went out of his way to let her know the identity of his current mistress. When she cleverly showed no anger but merely enquired whether she was as sexually attractive as her appearance suggested, Napoleon would be aroused to fury. He would ever justify his behaviour by insisting that he was no ordinary mortal and that moral and civic laws could not apply to him.

Invariably Josephine's refusal to adopt the role of the wronged wife brought Napoleon to heel. The mistress would be summarily dismissed and the tender beseeching husband would literally crawl into his wife's room, begging forgiveness and reconciliation. She never refused either.

Josephine was necessary to Napoleon not only emotionally but socially. The frantic steps he took to appear as an Emperor in the tradition of Charlemagne were really symptoms of the inferiority complex of a Corsican peasant. Some perversity of human nature made him discontented with the unique honours which he had obtained by military prowess and he sought avidly to earn the less commendable ones of veneration from his regal position.

He was perhaps conscious that by birth and by physique he could not ape the majesty of kings but he believed implicitly that Josephine was by nature a queen. In his adoring eyes her lowly birth, her chequered career, and her quite frequent lapses from what was the accepted social code, meant nothing. So great was his anxiety that she should be both pillar and prop in the role of Consort to an Emperor that he used to order her about as if she was an officer in his army.

'Tonight you will be dazzling in jewellery and richly dressed,' he would command. 'Do you hear me?'

Josephine would look at him quickly and reply:

'I will do my best, but you will countermand orders for payment of the bills of the jewels and dresses you are ordering me to wear.'

Napoeon's sense of humour would accept the justice of her remarks, at least for the time being. He would embrace her, saying:

'Certainly I sometimes cancel your warrants of payments because people impose upon your generous and easy nature and I cannot allow them to abuse you. But I am not inconsistent in ordering you to be magnificent on occasions of parade. One interest must be weighed against another. I hold the balance fairly.'

The conception that a social occasion was just like a military parade was typical of Napoleon's attitude to his wife at this period. She was becoming just a reliable general on his staff, albeit one that he found most attractive.

112

At the same time, he continually found fault with her extravagance. It seemed that she could not stop spending. She bought everything that was offered to her until there was nowhere to put anything new. Beautiful *objets d'art* were just looked at for a few minutes then left in a packing case or drawer.

Half of everything she bought she gave away to friends, relations or servants. A poor pensioner who came with a child to beg a little charity often left with a useless, extravagant plaything—an artificial orange tree, a monkey who played the violin or a bush of singing birds which Josephine had only fingered for a few seconds.

She had, as Empress, an annual income of 480,000 francs (nearly £20,000) payable monthly. In seven years she received an additional 2,000,000 francs to pay off her debts.

'Her extravagance,' Napoleon said at St. Helena, 'vexed me beyond measure. Calculating as I am, I would, of course, rather have given away a million francs than seen 100,000 squandered away.'

Josephine's day began with a bath—unlike her predecessor at the Tuileries, Marie Antoinette, who only washed those parts of her body not covered with clothes. This was followed by a toilet which took three hours. In a few years she spent on powders, lotions and rouge more than the purchase price of Malmaison. She possessed 600 hats, 676 cloth dresses and sixty cashmere shawls, the most beautiful of which cost from eight to ten thousand francs.

Masson writes of her jewels:

She possesses, according to an evaluation which is a third below the purchase-price, 4,354,255 francs' worth of valuable jewels, pearls and diamonds, and precious stones; but who can say how much has been paid for the thousands of objects in her keeping which she has worn perhaps once or not at all; the hundreds of rings, bracelets, girdle-buckles, necklaces of polished materials, and all kinds of beads, strings of agate, silver and gold, engraved stones, turquoise, malachite, scarabs, cut corals, corals with pearls . . . a number of them are merely

113

curiosities, dearly bought objects which have little or no sales-value. And then Josephine is always having the settings changed or modernised; she trades, buys, sells, exchanges, and takes for one stone ten others. . . . Among all these jewels, some of which must have reminded her of so many things, of events, of fame, of treasured and loved things, of the constant ascent of her star—of these ornaments, which were the ransoms of cities, of princes, of republics, gifts from popes and kings. New Year's presents, pledges of love, successive tokens which she should have kept, of all these things not one is left the way she received it. She defaces them, changes them, makes a girdle from a necklace from ear-rings pendants, she sends gold and silver to be melted down, orders stones according to her whims, and preserves in none of the jewels the memory connected with them. Where is the little filigree medallion, the erstwhile present of the Vendemiaire General to the Vicomtesse de Beauharnais? What has she done with this rarest and most valuable of all her ornaments? Oh, it is not worth anything, it does not sparkle: she has given it away with a handful of other things for a fashionable stone.

In May, 1805, Napoleon went to Italy to be crowned King there. He did not take Josephine with him and she was never anointed Queen of Italy. He made up for the rather pointed omission by making her son, Eugène, a Prince of the Empire and Arch-Chancellor of State.

Josephine did, however, consider it advisable to keep Napoleon within sight. She followed him at a discreet distance, making a tour of Northern Italy and visting the places which she had enjoyed years before.

After the ceremonies of the Coronation, Napoleon joined Josephine in Milan. He intended it to be a long holiday for them both. The idea had to be abandoned with the news of a new coalition of the powers against France which demanded Napoleon's immediate presence in Paris.

Back in the Tuileries Josephine spent a lonely and carefully supervised life.

'It would be better for me if I were the wife of a common labourer,' she told one of her ladies-in-waiting.

Napoleon did not often see her during this critical time; not even during the hour from four to five o'clock in the afternoon when he had been in the habit of visiting her while she rested in her room.

At night Josephine would force herself to remain awake sometimes until three o'clock in the morning. She would talk to one of her ladies but both knew that she was listening tensely for the familiar sound of the wardrobe door closing as Napoleon came down the private stairs.

He was, however, so busy with the preparations for his greatest military campaign that it was rare for him to find the time to return to his private apartments, even for sleep.

By autumn he was moving with his armies to the east. By the end of October he had won the battle of Ulm and had utterly destroyed the power of Austria. But at the same time that the news of this tremendous victory reached Paris there also came news of the complete defeat of the French Navy by Nelson at the battle of Trafalgar. Napoleon's dreams of world conquest were brought to nothing.

With redoubled fury he set out to destroy all opposition on the continent of Europe. On December 2nd, 1805, at Austerlitz the remnants of the Austrian forces and the major part of the army of their Russian allies were destroyed.

Josephine received news of these victories at Strasbourg, which was as close to the triumphant French forces as Napoleon permitted her to come. During this campaign there had been no problem of persuading her to leave Paris. She was only too anxious to be near him and to see what he was doing.

His letters at this time were still affectionate. They invariably ended with the words:

Adieu dear, I love you and embrace you.

But it naturally could not be expected that a long-married

115

man of thirty-seven should repeat the passion that he had shown in his letters within a few months of his marriage.

Josephine kept sending pleas that she be allowed to come nearer to him, particularly during the pause in the military campaign when Napoleon was living in Munich. He always put her off on the quite reasonable pretext that he would soon resume his march east and he did the same when he reached Vienna.

On October 27th he wrote to her:

> *Munich, October 27th, 1805*
>
> *I received your letter. . . . I was grieved to see how needlessly you have made yourself unhappy. I have heard particulars, which have proved how much you love me, but you should have more fortitude and confidence. Besides, I had advised you that I should be six days without writing you. . . . You must be cheerful, amuse yourself and hope that, before the end of the month, we shall meet.*
>
> *Adieu, my dear. Kindest regards to Hortense and Eugène.*

To indicate that he was not completely ignoring her wishes, he allowed her, in mid-November, to move to Munich where he arranged for a palace to be put at her disposal. This was really just a gesture, for the distance between them was as great as ever. Josephine was on her way to Munich when Napoleon won the greatest victory of his career at Austerlitz.

In Munich the Bavarians took good care to show their obedience to the French conqueror by fêting his wife with every possible means at their disposal.

For the first time Josephine met kings and queens on terms of equality. The gaiety went to her head and she was foolish enough to stop writing to Napoleon. Soon there were captious and somewhat sarcastic enquiries as to why she was too busy to answer his letters.

On December 10th he wrote:

> *It is a long time since I had news of you. Have the grand fêtes*

at Baden, Stuttgart and Munich made you forget the poor soldiers who live covered in mud, rain and blood? We are endeavouring to conclude peace. The Russians have gone and are in flight far from here; they are on their was back to Russia, well drubbed and very much humiliated. I am very anxious to be with you again.

Adieu, dear. My eyes are cured.

Nine days later he followed with a note:

December 19th

Great Empress,

Not a single letter from you since you left Strasbourg! You have gone to Baden, Stuttgart, and Munich without writing us a word. This is neither very kind nor very affection- ate. . . . The Russians are gone. I have a truce. In a few days I shall see what I may expect. Deign from the height of your grandeur to concern yourself a little with your slaves.

She fell back on the usual excuse that she had been unwell and Napoleon accepted her statement on its face value. He concluded the Peace of Pressburg and reached Munich on New Year's Day, 1806. For three weeks they were perfectly happy together.

Towards the end of January they set out for Paris. Napoleon wanted to travel alone at the greatest speed and Josephine to follow at her leisure. But she begged that they should go together.

'Well then,' he said at last, 'you will not have your usual migraine? If you promise me that, I will take you.'

She promised and although they travelled in the same carriage until they reached Fontainebleau she was well the whole time.

Once they were back in Paris Napoleon's sisters continued their campaign of hate against Josephine. Caroline suggested to her brother that he should prove to himself once and for all that he was capable of begetting a child.

Napoleon was tempted by her suggestion and allowed Caroline to introduce him to a young girl who had been deserted by her husband. She was very attractive, aged eighteen, and called Eléonore Denuelle de la Plaigne.

Despite the secrecy which surrounded all this intrigue Josephine heard about it. She wept when she heard that Eléonore was pregnant until her eyes were red and swollen and she spread gloom and despondency wherever she appeared.

When a new coalition of the remaining enemies of France—England, Russia and Prussia—was formed Napoleon went east once more. This time he took Josephine part of the way with him, for she absolutely refused to remain behind.

He installed her in a house at Mayence and on October 1st began his military campaign. A fortnight later he won the battle of Jena and in telling her of this triumph in a letter he stressed that it would be quite impossible to send for her.

He put her off time and time again because of the dangers and rigours of the journey. His thoughts were still with her with deep affection. He wrote, on November 1st, 1806:

Talleyrand has just arrived, and tells me, my dear, that you do nothing but cry. What on earth do you want? You have your daughter, your grandchildren, and good news; surely these are sufficient reasons for being happy and contented.

Josephine, in her unhappiness, started to try to learn her future from the cards. These were read by her lady-in-waiting, Madame de la Rochefoucauld—a hunchback—who was always pessimistic and full of gloomy foreboding.

Napoleon wrote on November 22nd:

I am sorry to find you in the dumps; yet you have every reason to be cheerful. You are wrong to show so much kindness to people who show themselves unworthy of it. Madame L. [la Rochefoucauld] is a fool; such an idiot that you ought to know her by this time and pay no heed to her. Be contented, happy in the influence you possess. In a few days I shall decide

118

whether to summon you here or send you to Paris.

On December 31st Napoleon learnt that Eléonore had given birth to a son. He wrote to Josephine:

I have had a good laugh over your last letters. You idealise the fair ones of Great Poland in a way they do not deserve. . . . I shrug my shoulders at the stupidity of Madame L.; still you show her your displeasure and advise her not to be so idiotic. Such things become common property and make many people indignant. For my part, I scorn ingratitude as the worst fault in a human heart. I know that, instead of comforting you, these people give you pain.

Madame de la Rochefoucauld's cards told Josephine that she would not be allowed to join Napoleon and that there was trouble everywhere, from every direction.

Josephine tried not to listen. Her boxes were packed, she was waiting only for Napoleon's permission to join him. On January 7th, 1807, Madame de la Rochefoucauld was proved right. Napoleon wrote:

I am pained by all you tell me; but the season being cold, the roads very bad and not at all safe, I cannot consent to expose you to so many fatigues and dangers. Return to Paris to spend the winter there. Go to the Tuileries, receive, and lead the same life as you are accustomed to do when I am there. That is my wish. . . . Believe that it costs me more than you to put off for some weeks the pleasure of seeing you.

Josephine would not believe that she could not join him. She wrote him two letters in the same day, imploring that she might come to him. He answered:

Paris claims you; go there, it is my wish.

Paris no longer held any attraction for Josephine. Not

only Madame de la Rochefoucauld's dark cards but her own instinct told her something was wrong. She wrote desperate, miserable letters, bespattered with the tears she could not control.

Napoleon wrote, on January 19th:

I am in despair, at the tone of your letter and at what I hear. I forbid you to weep, to be petulant and uneasy. I want you to to be cheerful, lovable and happy.

How could Josephine obey him? She had heard with terror the name, Marie Walewska.

10

Men always fall in love with the same type of woman so, Marie Walewska was, in many ways, a replica of Josephine.

All these fair Poles are Frenchwomen at heart, Napoleon had written in December.

Married to a bad-tempered man fifty years her senior, Marie Walewska at twenty-two was outstandingly beautiful even for a Polish woman of an aristocratic line. Blonde, tall and lissom she had, however, one attraction Josephine could no longer claim—youth.

Count Walewska was an elderly noble of distinguished Polish descent. Marie found life very boring. She was, however, extremely virtuous and she would not have surrendered herself to the conqueror of her country except for the fanatical patriotism of her Polish friends.

Napoleon first noticed this lovely young woman at a ball given in his honour in Warsaw.

'One might say,' he said later in recalling that moment, 'that her soul was as beautiful as her face. She was an angel.'

All that evening his eyes followed her.

'The day after the ball,' his valet reported, 'the Emperor seemed to be in an unusually agitated state. He walked about the room, sat down, got up and walked about again. Immediately after luncheon he sent a great person to visit Madame Walewska for him.'

The great person carried a note which was characteristic.

I have seen only you. I have admired only you, I desire only you. A very prompt answer to calm the impatient ardour of N.

There was little finesse about Napoleon's approaches. He was accustomed to command and for others to obey. Marie was not so amenable as the politicians.

Indignantly she showed the note to her friends and some of her relatives. They were members of the leading families of the country. For them one interest was paramount—Poland. They told Marie that it was in the interests of her country that she should yield.

Had she but known it—and only Josephine could have told her—the instinctive resistance she put up to Napoleon's advances when, at the behest of her patriotic relatives, she went to see him in private was precisely what was needed to fan a passing fancy into a passion. Although she did in time become Napoleon's devoted mistress her occasional coldness and resistance to his will helped to turn the Walewska affair into one of the great passions of Napoleon's life.

At that first meeting she found Napoleon waiting for her in a state of wild impatience and emotion.

'Every moment he enquired the time. Madame Walewska arrived at last, but in what a state—pale, dumb, her eyes bathed in tears.'

She poured out her troubles. Her unhappiness with her stern husband, her loneliness, her misery that the conqueror of her country should desire her!

She was pure and cold and she cried all the time but Napoleon was thrilled by her, and moved as he had never been moved before. He wrote the next morning:

Oh, give a little joy, a little happiness to a poor heart all ready to worship you. It is so difficult to get a reply. You owe me one.

N

She still wept and Napoleon wrote:

122

There are moments when too high rank is a burden, and that is what I feel. How can I satisfy the needs of a heart hopelessly in love, which would fling itself at your feet and which finds itself stopped by the weight of lofty considerations paralysing the most lofty desires. Oh, if you would! Only you could remove the obstacles that lie between us. My noble friend, Durot, will clear the way. Oh! Come! Come! All your wishes shall be gratified. Your native land will be dearer to me when you have had pity on my poor heart.

N

Few women, and certainly not a neglected young wife, could have been completely indifferent to the attentions of the leading figure in the world of his day.

Marie gave herself to the man who loved her, swearing that it was only for Poland's sake that she did so. Napoleon who had the delightful ability to forget his greatness became her beseeching, ardent lover. Writing with almost boyish adoration in a strain of idealism after their night together, he said:

Marie, my sweet Marie, my first thought is of you, my first desire is to see you again. You will come again, won't you? You promised you would. If you don't the eagle will fly to you! I shall see you at dinner—our friend tells me so. I want you to accept this bouquet: I want it to be a secret link, setting up a private understanding between us in the midst of the surrounding crowd. We shall be able to share our thoughts, though all the world is looking on. When my hand presses my heart, you will know that I am thinking of no one but you: and when you press your bouquet, I shall have your answer back! Love me, my pretty one, and hold your bouquet tight!

Josephine, hearing of the Marie Walewska affair, knew that her hold on her husband was weakening. Terribly significant to her was a letter which arrived in which he gave orders about the places she could, and could not, visit and who her friends should be.

The contents in themselves were no more than the Imperial commands she had become accustomed to receive and she did not mind the dictatorial tone nor even the absence of sentimental phrases. What did alarm her was that for the first time since she had known him Napoleon had dropped the affectionate '*tu*' for the coldly formal '*vous*'.

She protested about it, and Napoleon brushed off the change as a motiveless lapse. Probably it was. His infatuation for Marie was at its height and he doubtless dashed off his correspondence with only part of his attention given to the writing of it.

He treated the matter lightly in his reply, but '*tu*' was back in the subsequent letters, with protestations about his love and regrets that his destiny prevented him from having her with him as he would have wished.

Napoleon was at this time anxious that there should be no rift with Josephine. He was a long way from the seat of government; he had been away for months and it looked as if it would be as long before he could return. Josephine was invaluable as an emblem of his rule. She was one whom, with all her faults, he could trust more safely than the politicians of Paris. He told her that she must return to the French capital.

Warsaw, January 23rd, 1807
I have received your letter of 15th January. I can't possibly allow a woman to undertake the journey here. The roads are too bad—unsafe, and deep in mud. Go back to Paris; be happy and cheerful; and perhaps I will come soon. Your remark, that you married a husband in order to live with him, makes me smile. I thought, in my ignorance, that the wife was made for the husband, and the husband for the country, the family, and glory. Forgive my ignorance. There is always something one can learn from the fine ladies of to-day.

Good-bye, my dear. Remember how much it costs me not

to let you come. Say to yourself, 'It is a proof how precious I am to him'.

Napoleon

His anxiety to have Josephine in Paris was still the motive for refusing to allow her to come to Poland in the spring of 1807. The graphic descriptions of a hard, rough life in some primitive inn or an army camp with one of the Guards units did not impress Josephine.

There were Polish women in Paris who lost no time in telling her that Napoleon was very comfortably housed in the Castle of Finkenstein, where he had organised his military headquarters. The ladies were at pains to stress that Finkenstein was as big as many of the French châteaux Napoleon patronised and considerably more comfortable than most of them.

Marie Walewska was also established in the Polish castle. Josephine dared not challenge Napoleon by mentioning Marie by name. Instead she chided her husband about his brief and infrequent letters, suggesting that it must be because he had other ladies to write to. Napoleon saw a danger signal in this letter knowing Marie to be wildly, passionately in love with him, knowing that he found a satisfaction in their love greater then he had ever experienced except in his first months with Josephine. He sat down at his desk and insisted that there was only one woman in the world for him.

Finkenstein, 10th May, 1807

I have received your letter. I don't understand what you say about my lady correspondents. There is only one person I love, and that's my little Josephine. She's kind, she's capricious, she easily takes offence. Her quarrels are as graceful as everything she does: for she is always adorable, except when she is jealous, and then she becomes a regular little devil.

But to return to these ladies of yours. If I were to waste my time on any of them, you can be sure they would have to be pretty as rosebuds. Does that fit the ladies you mean?

*I want you never to dine with people who have not dined
with me. Keep to the same list for your private parties. Never
invite ambassadors or foreigners to Malmaison: I should be
angry with you if you did. And don't let yourself be imposed
upon by people whom I don't know, and who wouldn't come to
see you if I were there.*

Good-bye, my dear. All my love.

Napoleon

Temporarily Josephine's qualms were banished by tragedy.
The five-year-old Napoleon, her grandson, and son of
Hortense and Louis Bonaparte, died of diphtheria in the
Netherlands. The news came on May 7th, two days after the
child's death.

Josephine collapsed when she read the brief note and took
to her bed. Her strong maternal instincts had been revived by
the birth of her grandson. She adored the child even more
than her own two children. Little Napoleon's death had also
destroyed her hope that the blood of the La Pageries should
course throught the veins of Napoleon's successor.

Josephine was at St. Cloud. After she recovered from her
misery she requested permission from the Council of State to
ignore Napoleon's orders that she should stay in the Paris
region so that she could visit Hortense at The Hague.

Permission was granted for her to proceed as far as Brussels,
but no further. Hortense, with tearless, vacant eyes, met
Josephine at the Palace of Laeken. Josephine was uncannily
calm, moving like an automaton. She was numbed with
grief and deeply depressed with the hopelessness of her own
position.

Napoleon, knowing her as he did, knew what she would be
suffering and wrote:

Finkenstein, May 14th

*I realise the grief which the death of this poor Napoleon must
cause you; you can imagine what I am enduring. I should like
to be by your side in order that your sorrow might be kept within*

*reasonable bounds. You have had the good fortune never to
lose children, but it is one of the pains and conditions attached
to our miseries here below. I trust I may hear you have been
rational in your sorrow and that your health remains good.
Would you willingly augment my grief?*

On May 20th he said:

*I am sorry to see that you have not been rational. Grief has
bounds which should not be passed. Take care of yourself for
the sake of your friend and believe in my entire affection.*

From Marienburg on June 3rd he wrote:

*Every letter that comes from St. Cloud tells me you are
always weeping. That is not well; it is necessary for you to
keep well and cheerful. Hortense is still unwell; what you tell
me of her makes me very sorry for her.*

There is no doubt that Josephine's prolonged melancholy
was based on her physical health at this time. She was naturally
gay and bright; she wept easily and smiled a moment or two
later. This long drawn out unhappiness was, in part, due to
the beginnings of the change of life and secondly to the fact
that she was suffering from septic poisoning.

Her teeth had been getting worse and now people who were
close to her complained that her breath smelt.

She wept also because she was afraid of the future. The
campaign in the east was over. The Tsar had obediently
signed the Treaty of Tilsit with Napoleon who was making
plans to return to France. A letter written at Dresden told
her:

*One of these fine nights I may turn up at St. Cloud in the role
of the jealous husband: I give you fair warning. Good-bye, my
dear. It will be a great pleasure to see you. All my love.*

Napoleon came bustling home full of his victories, but nothing was said about divorce. Josephine felt unutterably relieved as though she feared that he was merely waiting a favourable opportunity.

Then she learnt of what might be a very different explanation. Surprised that Marie Walewska was not pregnant, Napoleon had wrung from Eléonore the confession that Murat, as well as he, had been her lover.

Josephine's self-confidence returned, but it was short-lived.

Probably the most devastating blow she received was a formal order to her that in future, both in private and public, she was to address her husband as 'Sire'. She was being given no more privileges of familiarity than the lowliest subject in the Empire.

The obvious situation was duly noted by those who had previously found friendship with Josephine expedient and profitable. Fouché ceased to pay her a retaining fee for information. Even Murat, her one-time lover, cold-shouldered her. These fairweather friends increased their gestures of friendship to Napoleon and their advice to him was to seek a divorce without delay.

There came the day when an *aide-de-camp* approached Josephine and told her that the Emperor wished her to attend him in his private apartments.

He strode up and down, not looking at her.

'The death of little Napoleon Charles,' he said, 'is a tragedy for you, my dear; a tragedy for France; above all, a tragedy for me.'

He came across and sat a yard or two away from her before he went on:

'The situation may be forced upon me to ensure that an heir—a legitimate heir—should be born. It may well become inevitable that a divorce should be arranged and a marriage take place for reasons of State.'

Despite his determination to treat the business merely as a State matter his voice began to break with emotion as he touched Josephine's arm, and went on:

128

'If such a thing came to pass, Josephine, it would be your duty to help me to make such a sacrifice. I should count on your friendship to preserve me from the odium of this forced separation. I am confident that you would take the first step, wouldn't you? And putting yourself in my place you would have the courage to decide upon your retirement?'

Josephine was trembling a little as she thought over her answer. She was fighting hard for the first time in her life to hide her emotions instead of parading them.

'Sire, you are my master and you will decide upon my fate,' she said at length. 'When you order me to leave the Tuileries I shall obey at once, but the order must come from you. I am your wife. I have been crowned by you in the presence of the Pope. The worth of such honours is such that one cannot give them up of one's own free will. If you divorce me all France must know that is it you who drive me away, and people shall not be unaware either of my obedience or of my profound sorrow.'

She could stand no more. Without waiting for permission to withdraw, as Napoleon had recently insisted she must do before she left him, she went blindly to the door. The tears were pouring down her cheeks.

Gossip-hungry courtiers and ladies in attendance soon extracted from her every detail of the interview. She cried unceasingly and in outbursts of anger she revealed intimate details of Napoleon's infidelity to whoever would listen.

There were few people who could find any enjoyment in gloating over the pathetic, unhappy situation in which this forty-four-year-old woman found herself.

'I will never give way to him,' she cried pathetically. 'I shall certainly show myself his victim. But if I end by causing him too much annoyance, who knows of what he is capable, and whether he will resist the temptation to put me out of the way?'

People repeated excitedly that Josephine suspected the Emperor of foul play and naturally he heard what was being said. In the winter of 1807 he remarked to Lucien:

'Josephine is getting old and as she can't have any children she is very melancholy about it and tiresome. She fears divorce and even worse. Just imagine, the woman cries every time she has indigestion because she says she has been poisoned by those who want me to marry someone else. It is detestable!'

The murmurings in official circles were such that Napoleon deemed it wise to defer definite action. The emergence of a pro-Josephine faction was not so much an indication of any personal liking for her but of strong suspicions about a Bonaparte Royal line in a country which had suffered much to get rid of a Bourbon dynasty. There were many who thought that if any monarchy returned at all it might as well be the old one.

The result was that during the summer and autumn Josephine enjoyed the full glory of appearing as the Emperor's devoted consort. She was second only to Napoleon in precedence at the ostentatious wedding of Jerome Bonaparte to Catherine of Württemberg; she was hostess to the Imperial guests at the Rambouillet hunting box and subsequently at Fontainebleau.

The latter was a great occasion. Napoleon organised his guests' activities as if they were on parade.

'It is curious,' he remarked naively. 'I gathered at Fontainebleau a great number of people. I wanted them to be amused. I arranged all their entertainments—and everyone has a weary, melancholy air.'

Josephine, who had just heard that her mother had died in Martinique, made no effort to amuse the party. Without her sure hand the festivities fell flat. Even when Napoleon began a blatant *liaison* with her new reader, an Italian, named Madame Gazzani, she felt too despondent to make a protest.

Fouché misjudged the situation. He thought that Josephine was miserable because Napoleon had already told her that he would put divorce proceedings in motion as soon as they returned to Paris To consolidate his position with Napoleon he saw Josephine alone and said, after some preamble:

'You should ask the Senate to join you in begging the Emperor to divorce you. What sacrifice is too great for the general good of France and for the consolidation of the dynasty?'

'You do not come at the Emperor's bidding?' Josephine demanded.

'No,' admitted Fouché.

'Then I am not accountable to you,' Josephine retorted. 'I regard my marriage as recorded in the book of Destiny. I have no comments for you and will never do anything except with the Emperor's specific order.'

She refused to sign the document he had brought with him and Fouché slunk out of the room, alarmed that he had played his cards so badly. Napoleon noted the seething hostility between Josephine and Fouché and set enquiries on foot to discover the reason. Told that he was alleged to have repudiated his wife privately as a preliminary to a public separation he was extremely angry. He comforted Josephine and resumed cohabitation with her, but at the same time asked her to express her opinion on the matter of divorce.

Josephine wrote a letter which owed its inspiration to Talleyrand whose suggestions were relayed to her by her lady-in-waiting, Madame de Rémusat.

I will never take the first steps to bring about a change which must separate me from you. Our destiny has been so extraordinary that it has certainly been directed by Providence. I believe it would bring misfortune on both of us if, of my own accord, I tried to separate my life from yours.

Josephine's power over Napoleon was so strong that he offered to dismiss Fouché and actually wrote an official memorandum to him ordering him to cease meddling in his private affairs.

Fouché dutifully spread the report that rumours of an impending divorce were greatly exaggerated and bided his time for revenge on Josephine.

131

The chance came quite soon. When Napoleon left for Italy in November to organise a blockade in the Mediterranean against the English naval forces Josephine, possibly in the reaction from the strain of the past ten months, reverted to something of her old self.

Among the guests at Fontainbleau had been the handsome and youthful German Prince of Mecklenburg-Schwerin. After Napoleon's departure and the general exodus of the guests who had been at Fontainebleau the Prince was invited to stay on in Paris. Josephine enjoyed his company and was unwise enough to go with him incognito to the theatre. Fouché's agents of course reported the matter and the Chief of Police took good care that it was in turn reported to Napoleon.

He reprimanded her, not for any possible infidelity, but for behaviour unseemly in an Empress.

'You must not go to small boxes at small theatres,' he warned her. 'It does not become your rank. You must go only to the four principal theatres and always to the principal box.'

Josephine took little notice of the advice. She continued to enjoy herself. Her confidence was strengthened by the knowledge that Fouché had again been reproved for his activities.

I observe with pain, Napoleon had written to him, *that according to your reports people continue to discuss matters which must distress the Empress and are unseemly from all points of view.*

Fouché's efficient espionage service, which had enabled him to send a detailed résumé of everything Josephine did or said, had failed to have the expected impact. The likelihood of a divorce seemed to be receding. Napoleon and Josephine were apparently drifting into the quiet waters of middle-aged contentment and tolerance, each of the other.

The emergence from the dark days of despair encouraged Josephine to claim:

'I am at the summit of my joy.'

It was an exaggeration and a challenge but justified as a boast to counteract the prophecies of her enemies and to prove to the world her hold on Napoleon was as strong as ever.

11

The blow that Josephine had expected was not, however, to fall for a time. In the first few weeks of 1808, to her surprise, she found Napoleon both considerate and affectionate. Marie Walewska seemed to have been almost forgotten and he was constantly demanding that his wife should be near him.

The ceaseless round of dinners and parties was the cause of minor ailments to his digestive system which caused him considerable pain. Whenever he felt really ill he became rather like a pathetic little boy. He would hurry through the crowded reception rooms calling for Josephine.

When he found her, he would lay his head on her shoulder and ask to be comforted. On one occasion when he was ill and Josephine came to him, he caught her in his arms crushing her dress and sobbed:

'My poor Josephine! No, I can never leave you.'

The faction which avidly desired Napoleon to divorce his wife was always furious at these examples of what seemed to be a reconciliation and never more so when Josephine managed to persuade him to go to bed.

Napoleon would only agree to do so if she would come as well. This, of course, she did and though she never said anything, her air of triumph was not lost on those guests who had hitherto insisted that the married life of the Emperor and Empress was over.

'What a devil of a man!' Talleyrand cried angrily. 'He gives way constantly to his first impulse and doesn't know what he wants to do. Let him make up his mind, and not leave us to be the mere sport of his words, not knowing really on what footing we are with him.'

The period of social pleasure, which was appealing more and more to Napoleon, ceased abruptly when there was trouble regarding the succession in Spain. Political dissension among the members of the Spanish Royal Family gave Napoleon the excuse to put his brother Joseph on the throne. To Josephine's surprise and delight, Napoleon asked her to accompany him at least as far as Bordeaux.

Soon after he had left her at Bordeaux he wrote:

April 17th, 1808

It took me some time to understand your little jokes: I have laughed at your recollections. Oh, you women, what memories you have!

My health is fairly good, and I love you most affectionately. I wish you to give my kind regards to everybody at Bordeaux; I have been too busy to send them to anybody.

Six days later he summoned Josephine to join him at Bayonne. She wrote to her daughter Hortense:

You can imagine that it is a great happiness for me not to be away from the Emperor, so I am off tomorrow early.

At Bayonne the Spanish Court as well as Spanish and French politicians were among Napoleon's guests, but he seemed strangely lackadaisical about pushing his political schemes ahead, preferring to spend his time with his wife.

It was spring and the weather was lovely. The years seemed to evaporate and Napoleon became his old boyish self. The Royal guests and the motley crowd of *aides* and ladies-in-waiting were dumbfounded one day. They were strolling along the seashore from the Château of Marrac when Napoleon whispered something to Josephine, who giggled and promptly rushed away with her husband after her, chasing her pell-mell across the sands.

When he managed to manoeuvre her so that she was close

135

to the edge of the water he pushed her in and plunged in after her. Laughing so that they could hardly get to their feet, the two of them came romping over the sands until they stopped breathless and dripping with water before their guests.

On another occasion when they went along the coast in a procession of carriages, Josephine asked Napoleon to halt. She then took off her shoes and went paddling. Napoleon carried her shoes for her, and when she got back to the carriage threw them into a thorn bush, declaring that he would simply love to see the faces of the Court when she had to walk barefoot into the Château.

One possible reason for Napoleon's attentiveness to his wife at this time was that on the 23rd April Josephine had received news from her daughter Hortense that she had given birth to a healthy son. The birth of this child made it possible for Napoleon to reconsider an arrangement whereby his grandson became his official heir.

The general atmosphere of happiness was augmented by a settlement of the Spanish succession. Joseph was to be head of the Spanish reigning house—Napoleon believed this to be a triumph.

With the matter settled to his satisfaction, Napoleon made a leisurely return with Josephine towards Paris.

Hardly had they reached Toulouse than a message came of a Spanish revolt. Within days further news arrived reporting that Joseph had fled from Madrid and a French army of 20,000 men had been surrounded and taken prisoner.

'This means,' Napoleon said grimly, 'that I must conquer Spain or abandon it.'

The remainder of the journey to Paris found the Emperor a preoccupied and sullen-tempered man with little time to devote to his wife. He knew that he would have personally to direct military operations in Spain but, before he began them, he must make certain that there was no possibility of an attack on France by the country's erstwhile enemies across the Rhine.

Josephine had deep forebodings about the way the political situation was developing and she said as much to Napoleon.

136

He was perhaps the more annoyed because he knew that what she said was true.

It is a reflection on his military genius that even his wife should prophesy disaster, and he categorically rejected her offer to be by his side during the troublous times ahead.

Josephine wept bitterly at being left behind but this time ineffectively. She had therefore to remain in Paris while Napoleon went off to Erfurt, where he obtained the approval of Tsar Alexander of Russia and of the Germanic Kings and Princes to invade Spain without any interference from them.

Napoleon got on well with the Tsar and confessed to him that he was deeply unhappy about Josephine's inability to bear him childern. He admitted that he was urgently considering the matter of divorce—a piece of news which was not, of course, unknown to Alexander who was already considering the possibility of selling one of his unmarried sisters as a consort for the French Emperor in return for a guarantee of Russia's western frontiers.

In the Tuileries Josephine awaited news of the conference at Erfurt with growing anxiety. Her own political connections had informed her of the Tsar's schemes as regards marrying off his sister and she knew that even if she could entrance Napoleon when she was near him so that all question of divorce was forgotten, the moment he was away from her he not only looked around for mistresses but constantly occupied his mind with thoughts of his succession.

Her worries were by no means minimised by the cheerful letters which Napoleon sent her, in one of which he said:

I assisted at the Weimar Ball. The Emperor Alexander dances, but not I. Forty years are forty years.

However, his next letter struck a chill to her heart.

My dear,

      I write you seldom, I am very busy. Conversations

which last whole days and which do not improve my cold. Still,
all goes well. I am pleased with Alexander; he ought to be with
me. If he were a woman I think I should make him my sweet-
heart.

I shall be back to you shortly; keep well and let me find you
plump and rosy.

Josephine, miserable and agitated, imagined how easy it
would be for Napoleon to find a feminine member of the
Russian Royal Family as delightful as he apparently found
the Emperor Alexander.

Superficially the conference at Erfurt was a Napoleonic
triumph and on the Emperor's return to Paris he was cock-a-
hoop with the certainty of success. He stopped at the Tuileries
for only a few days before departing to lead his armies
against Spain.

Josephine was almost beside herself with apprehension
as to the outcome. Her frantic attempts to go with her husband
were motivated as much by fears for his personal safety as
by any wish to safeguard her own position as his wife.

'Will you never stop making war?' Josephine cried.

'Do you think I enjoy it?' he asked. 'Don t you think I
would rather stay peaceably where I have a good bed and a
good dinner instead of facing all the hardships I have before
me? You think I am made differently from other men?
Then I can do other things besides wage war. But needs must. I
owe a duty to France. It is not I who direct the course of
events. I obey it.'

Although time and time again Napoleon had abruptly
refused to take Josephine with him, on the morning of his
departure she rushed down the steps as he conferred with
his officers and clung to him as he moved towards his carriage.
She was still clinging to the door handle as Napoleon ordered
the driver to whip the horses to a gallop.

All Josephine's premonitions about the new campaign
proved to be correct. For the first time in Napoleon's career
the French people were divided. A very large section, weary of

war, had little enthusiasm and even actual hatred for this new campaign to keep Joseph Bonaparte in Madrid by force of arms. But at first Napoleon's military skill brought a veneer of success and his letters to Josephine were cheerful and reassuring.

December 31st, 1808

The last few days I have been in pursuit of the English, but they fled panic stricken.

January 3rd, 1809

My dear, I have received your letters of the 18th and 21st. I am close behind the English.

A happy New Year and a very happy one to my Josephine.

As ever he began to miss her and he could foreshadow personal happiness for them.

I shall be in Paris the moment I think it worthwhile. I warn you to beware of ghosts. One fine night at two in the morning! But adieu, my dear. I am well and am yours ever.

Napoleon

However, when Napoleon did return to Paris, Austria, taking advantage of his war in Spain to open hostilities on her ancient enemy, left him little time for love-making. Dislike for the Spanish war had given birth to political intrigue in the French capital so that in the event of Napoleon's death—whether naturally in war or by assassination it was not mentioned—Murat, now King of Naples, would be elected head of the French Empire.

These enemies of Napoleon were automatically Josephine's enemies as well, not only because of her devotion to her husband, which was very different from her somewhat doubtful allegiance in the years before, but because they feared that her own amazing tolerance of Napoleon's waywardness would enable her to outwit their intrigues.

She had let it be known that she was perfectly agreeable for either of Napoleon's illegitimate sons, one by Marie

Walewska and the other by Mademoiselle Dennelle, to be adopted by her and thereby become his legitimate heirs.

In mid-April Napoleon left to take command of his armies on the eastern side of the Rhine. Gone was the triumphant and carefree atmosphere of the spring in the previous year.

Partly to take Josephine away from the intrigues in the capital and also to quieten her, he agreed that she should accompany him as far as Strasbourg, where he left her to launch his brief and highly successful campaign against the Austrians.

Josephine remained at Strasbourg for a short time, but feeling unwell gained Napoleon's permission in June to take the waters at Plombières, which had become her favourite holiday resort.

He wrote to her there on June 19th, saying:

I am glad that the Grand Duke of Berg is with you. Adieu dear. You know what my affection is, my Josephine; it never varies.

On July 7th he wrote at 5 a.m. from Ebersdorf and added:

I am sunburnt. Adieu dear. I send you a kiss.

In August Josephine returned to Malmaison where she received the news of Napoleon's succession of victories which culminated in the decisive engagement at Wagram.

She expected that he would then return to France. She began dreaming of ways in which she could effect a real reconciliation, either by the adoption of his illegitimate sons or by making him confirm publicly that Hortense's little boy should become his heir.

One day when the Duchesse d'Abrantés took her little daughter to see the Empress, Josephine said brokenly:

'You can have no idea how much I have suffered when any one of you has brought a child to me! Heaven knows that I am not envious, but in this case I have felt as if a deadly poison were creeping through my veins when I have looked upon the fresh and rosy cheeks of a beautiful child, the joy of its mother, but above all, the hope of its father! Yet God is my witness that I love him more than my life, and much more than that throne, that crown which he has given me!'

Napoleon's letters from Austria were genial.

> *Schoenbrunn, August 26th, 1809*
>
> *I have your letter from Malmaison. They bring me word that you are plump, florid and in the best of health. I assure you Vienna is not an amusing city. I would very much rather be back again in Paris.*

> *Schoenbrunn, August 31st*
>
> *I have had no letter from you for several days; the pleasures of Malmaison, the beautiful greenhouses, the beautiful gardens, cause the a bsent to be forgotten. It is, they say, the rule of your sex.*

> *Schoenbrunn, September 25th*
>
> *I have received your letter. Be careful, and I advise you to be vigilant, for one of these nights you will hear a loud knocking.*

Napoleon's excuse for not returning for a long time was the perfectly justifiable one that the peace negotiations were intricate and prolonged. But the truth was his determination to select a bride who would not only be the mother of his children but a valuable symbol of political alliance.

To his fury his idea of marrying one of the Emperor Alexander's sisters came to nothing. This was thanks to the loathing of the Russian Dowager Empress. She regarded Napoleon as a common upstart and a bloody tyrant. The old lady promptly got one daughter—Catherine—out of the way by marrying her to Prince George of Oldenburg. The Grand Duchess Anne she stated categorically was far too young for marriage and persuaded Alexander to agree.

With the possibility of marriage temporarily in abeyance, Napoleon decided to return to France. The peace treaty was signed on October 14th, and on October 21st he addressed a cold and formal note to Josephine.

My dear, I leave in one hour's time. I shall arrive at Fontaine-bleau on the 26th. or 27th. Meet me there with your ladies.

This note was sent from Munich and reached Josephine at St Cloud three days later. She had moved to St. Cloud from Malmaison in the belief that her husband would soon be returning to Paris but she had not expected him to be back in French territory so soon.

The brevity of the note and the command that the ladies of the Court should be present when they met were ominous. Josephine recognised that the blow was to fall at last. In a sudden panic she felt she could not face it. She imagined that Napoleon could not possibly be at Fontainebleau before the evening of the 26th at the earliest. In point of fact, he arrived at breakfast time on that morning and found nobody in the Palace to receive him.

He immediately sent a peremptory order to St. Cloud for Josephine. Hortense wrote in her memoirs:

The Emperor arrived at Fontainebleau and sent us word to join him there. My Mother, instead of being delighted, felt her heart sink.

Josephine delayed on one pretext and another before making the journey so that actually she did not reach Fontaine-bleau until shortly before six o'clock in the evening.

Napoleon, who had been pacing restlessly up and down all day, continually pulling out his watch and exhibiting outbursts of bad temper, saw her coach approaching and immediately went to the library, pretending to write.

Josephine had expected him to receive her in the hall or in the main reception room and stood around there with her ladies. Eventually she went upstairs to the library on the first floor and entered the room.

142

Napoleon looked up briefly from his desk.

'So you have come, Madame,' he said harshly. 'It is high time. I was about to set out for St. Cloud.'

He pretended to resume his writing. Josephine stood looking at him, the tears running down her cheeks.

The storm broke. Napoleon had meant to be calm and dignified but he had never been good at waiting. This time the strain swept away all restraint.

He raged and shouted his reproaches and complaints while Josephine's sobs grew louder and louder.

Finally, his anger exhausted, he made some attempt to comfort her and suggested that she changed for dinner.

Josephine retired to her own apartments and was soon in tears again. In the previous weeks, on Napoleon's secret instructions the communicating door between her own suite and that of the Emperor had been bricked up.

On the gentle and sympathetic encouragement of her ladies, she washed her face, put on even more make-up than usual and dressed herself in a gown that she had had made especially for the occasion. She knew that she looked really beautiful but when she went down to the banqueting room all that Napoleon did was to mutter:

'Your toilet has taken an hour and a half, Madame.'

The meal was a formal one, for some of Napoleon's Ministers had arrived and the talk was solely of political matters. After dinner was over both Napoleon and Josephine retired to their rooms, Josephine to lie awake for many hours and staring at the still fresh plaster where once had been an open door.

All Napoleon's Ministers expected that he would now acquaint Josephine with his decision to have a divorce and indeed he had informed some of his more intimate friends that he had definitely made up his mind to do so. During his military campaign he had found it impossible to put the words in writing, determining to tell Josephine in person what he intended to do.

Josephine certainly did not make things easier for him. She wept without ceasing behind closed doors.

Napoleon spent the days out driving with his sister Paolina, the Princess Borghese. He also visited her every evening. Most people guessed that the reason was a very attractive Piedmontese lady in the Princess's service.

But Josehine started the rumour that Napoleon was committing incest with his sister.

A fortnight slipped by and still Napoleon had not been able to speak a word about divorce. On November 14th the Court returned to the Tuileries, but things were no better. Whenever Napoleon was alone with Josephine she burst into loud sobbings and he was unable to make himself heard.

Only once did he manage to beg her to take the initiative and ask him to sacrifice her for the good of France.

'It's not the throne that I mind losing,' she cried bitterly, 'it's you—my husband, my lover, my all!'

Napoleon was touched.

'Do not try to move me,' he begged. 'I still love you, but in politics it is a case of head and not heart. I will give you five millions a year and a principality with Rome as its capital. Do you think that this divorce will be the event of my life? What a scene for a tragedy!'

Everyone was waiting for the fatal step to take place. Napoleon's mother, Madame Mère, who had always disliked Josephine, said to Madame Junot:

'I hope the Emperor will have the courage this time to take the step which not only France, but all Europe, awaits with anxiety. His divorce is a necessary act.'

On November 30th, 1809, Napoleon and Josephine dined together but hardly spoke a word to each other. Immediately after the coffee had been served Napoleon asked Josephine to come into his study. He shut the door behind her and she saw his face was, in her own words, 'set like the face of a statue'.

'Josephine, my lovely Josephine,' he said. 'You know how much I have loved you; that to you, to you alone, I owe the little happiness I have experienced in this world. But, Josephine, my destiny is more powerful than my will; my dearest

144

affections must yield to the interests of France. . . .'

He had expected tears but not the piercing shriek which Josephine gave as she threw herself on the floor.

'I shall not survive it. . . . I shall not survive it,' she screamed.

Bausset, who had been on duty in the dining room, ran to the door of the room.

'Suddenly,' he says, 'I heard loud cries proceeding from the Emperor's drawing room and emitted by the Empress Josephine. The usher, thinking that she was ill, was about to open the door, but I prevented him, saying that the Emperor would call for help if he thought right. I was standing near the door when Napoleon opened it, and perceiving me said hastily:

' "Come in, Bausset, and shut the door."

'I entered the drawing room and saw the Empress lying on the floor uttering piercing cries.

' "I shall not survive it!" she kept repeating.

'Napoleon said to me:

' "Are you strong enough to lift Josephine and carry her to her apartments by the private staircase communicating with her room so that she may have all the care and attention her state requires?"

'With Napoleon's help I raised her in my arms, and he, taking a candlestick off the table, lighted me and opened the door of the drawing room. When we reached the head of the staircase, I pointed out to him that it was too narrow for me to carry her down without running the risk of a fall. Napoleon called an attendant, gave him the candle, and himself took hold of Josephine's legs to help me to descend more gently. When she felt the efforts I was making to save myself from falling she said in a low voice:

' "You are holding me too tightly."

'I then saw that I need be under no uneasiness as to her health and that she had not lost consciousness for a moment. The Emperor's agitation and anxiety were extreme. In his trouble he told me the cause of all that had occurred. His words came out with difficulty and without sequence; his

145

voice was choked and his eyes were full of tears. . . . The whole scene did not last more than seven or eight minutes. Napoleon sent instantly to fetch Corvoisart [his doctor], Queen Hortense, Cambacérès and Fouché, and before returning to his own room he went to assure himself of Josephine's state and found her more calm and resigned.'

Coming out of the room Napoleon met Hortense.

'Go to her, daughter,' he said. 'Keep up courage.'

'Oh, Sire,' Hortense replied, 'I have courage.'

Napoleon was so upset and pertubed by what had occurred that Bausset was quite alarmed about him.

He wept again the next day when he heard that Hortense and Eugène proposed to accompany their mother when she left.

'What! All of you leave me!' he cried in a broken voice. 'You will desert me! Don't you love me any longer? If it were my happiness I would sacrifice it to you. But it is for the good of France. Pity me rather for being obliged to sacrifice my most cherished affections.'

Josephine was by now well enough to put forward large demands for the future. Her debts were enormous and she knew that she must press for a large settlement.

'Every day brought for her conflicts,' Hortense said miserably.

Napoleon was now as hysterical as Josephine. He swore he would not be left alone, while Josephine, turn by turn, wept and screamed and fainted. At last he announced what he was prepared to do for them all.

Josephine was to keep her Imperial and Royal rank and title. She was to receive an annual income of £80,000 from the public Treasury and £40,000 a year from his privy purse.

'We were won over by the Emperor's solicitude for his wife's reputation,' says Hortense. 'Already we were prepared to accept the new position which placed us on an equality with the crowd that we had seen at our feet and reduced us to be of no account where once we had been so influential.'

What made Josephine pull herself together more than anything else was the triumph and delight of the Bonapartes.

146

They had always hated her and they did not attempt to disguise their joy that the divorce was now almost an accomplished fact.

On the first of December she went with Napoleon to hear the *Te Deum* in Notre Dame which marked the anniversary of the Coronation. She was also present at the official receptions.

Her courage and dignity made a great impression and she received demonstrations of sympathy on all sides.

I can never forget, says Pasquier, the evening on which the discarded Empress did the honours of her Court for the last time. . . . A great throng was present and supper was served according to custom, in the gallery of Diana on a number of little tables. Josephine sat at the centre one, and the men went round her waiting for that particularly graceful nod which she was in the habit of bestowing on those with whom she was acquainted. I stood at a short distance from her for a few minutes, and I could not help being struck by the perfection of her attitude in the presence of all these people who still did her homage, while knowing full well that it was for the last time; that in an hour she would descend from the throne, and leave the palace never to re-enter it. Only women can rise superior to the difficulties of such a situation, but I have my doubts as to whether a second one could have been found to do it with such perfect grace and composure. Napoleon did not show as bold a front as did his victim.

Josephine was playing a difficult part magnificently and she was determined that she would not allow herself to be humiliated at the official ceremony of divorce, which took place at the Tuileries.

All the Bonapartes were there gloating at reaching the culmination of all their hopes and intrigues. Madame Mère hard as a rock; Caroline, Queen of Naples, and her husband Murat who had been Josephine's lover; Pauline beautiful and debauched; Lucien sinister and sarcastic; Jerome, now King of Westphalia, and his wife, and Louis, King of Holland.

Napoleon had done everything he could to make the ceremony, not one of dismissal of a culpable wife, but of an honourable renunciation by both in which each could be shown to be making a noble self-sacrifice.

Josephine was almost unnaturally calm. She had dressed herself in a white gown without a single touch of colour and no jewellery beyond her wedding ring. The seats for the witnesses had been arranged in a huge semi-circle in the Throne Room. As they filed in they saw the Emperor and Empress standing hand-in-hand.

Napoleon spoke first.

'The political interests of my monarchy,' he began, 'and the desires of my people, which have constantly guided my actions, require that I should leave behind me, to heirs of my love for my people, the throne upon which Providence has placed me. For many years I have given up all hope of children by my marriage with my deeply loved wife, the Empress Josephine. This is what induces me to sacrifice the sweetest desires of my heart, to consider only the good of my subjects, and to desire a dissolution of our marriage.

'I am now forty, and I may reasonably hope to live long enough to rear and guide any children which it may please God to grant me. Heaven knows what the decision has cost me, but there is no sacrifice, however great, which I would not make in the interests of France.

'It is my duty to add that I have no cause for complaint; on the contrary I have nothing but praise for the gentle and devoted love of my wife. She has enriched fifteen years of my life; their memory will be always engraved on my heart.

'She was crowned by my hand; she shall always retain the rank and title of Empress. Above all it is my hope that she shall never doubt my love for her, nor regard me as anything but her greatest and closest friend.'

Despite the pomposity and official flavour of the speech the words certainly came from Napoleon's heart and his voice was at breaking point when he ended; his eyes were filled with tears.

It was now Josephine's turn to speak. Moving a little away from Napoleon, she held the sheets of her own private notepaper on which the words had been written in her own handwriting and adapted from the speech written for her to include her own sentiments.

She began in a clear and strong voice, the tones as beautiful as ever.

'With the permission of our august and dear husband,' she said, 'I declare that since I have no hope of bearing children who can meet the requirements of the Emperor's policy in the interests of France it is my pleasure to give him the greatest proof of attachment and devotion that was ever given by woman on earth.'

The voice faltered and stopped. For a few moments there was utter silence as everyone sat waiting for her to continue. She stared at the paper and her lips moved but no sound came.

Gently, Count Regnaud, secretary of the Imperial Household, took the sheets from her and began reading the rest of the speech on her behalf. It sounded formal and empty without the enrichment of that vibrant, unbelievably attractive voice which had entranced even those who were her enemies.

The ceremony had taken place quite late in the evening and when Josephine's speech was ended there remained only the signing of the official report of the occasion by all the witnesses present. Before this was completed, Josephine had left the Throne Room accompanied by her two children.

Apart from being unable to complete her speech, she had kept herself under excellent control and even when her son Eugène fainted at the end of the ceremony, she remained impassive. But after her ladies had prepared her for bed and she had assured Hortense that she would be all right, the full impact of what had happened in the past hour swept over her.

She looked across the room and saw the secret door which led to Napoleon's bedroom. With tears streaming down her cheeks, she went across to the door, tiptoed up the stairs and burst into the Emperor's bedroom. He had already retired and was half asleep when he heard the noise of the wardrobe door opening.

Josephine appeared. She came slowly to the bedside, her eyes closed as if she was walking in her sleep. She reached the bed and fell forward throwing her arms around Napoleon, crying noisily.

Napoleon tried to comfort her with promises of friendship and appeals to her courage.

It was with difficulty that he restrained his own tears, and an hour passed before he led her back to the wardrobe and watched her take the stairs to her own room. It was the last time that Josephine was to sleep in the Tuileries in the bed of Marie Antoinette.

Napoleon had decided to live at the Petit Trianon at Versailles—the little palace Marie Anotinette had loved. He was ready to leave the next morning and the carriages were at the door. Suddenly he turned to his secretary.

'Meneval, come with me.'

He opened a secret door in his study and led the way by a winding staircase to Josephine's apartments. He went in. Josephine was alone, weeping miserably. She jumped up, flung herself into his arms.

'He pressed her to his bosom,' says Meneval, 'kissing her over and over again. But in the excess of her emotion she had fainted. I ran to the bell and summoned help. The Emperor, wishing to avoid the sight of a grief he was unable to assuage, placed the Empress in my arms as soon as he saw she was coming back to consciousness, ordered me not to leave her, and withdrew rapidly by the drawing rooms of the ground floor at the door of which his carriage was waiting for him.'

At 2 p.m. Josephine came down the grand staircase. The servants came from the kitchens to bid her good-bye.

Everyone was crying and outside in the streets and cafés people shook their heads. Josephine was still 'Our Lady of Victories'. Nothing, they said, would be the same now she had gone. To them she represented all that was kind and gentle and merciful. Without her there was only the iron hand and the discipline of Napoleon.

With the tears running down her cheeks Josephine left the palace for ever. It was pouring with torrential rain which seemed a fitting background to her misery.

'It is the end,' she said, 'the end of me.'

12

Napoleon spent a restless and unhappy night. Foolishly
he opened the wounds by rushing over the next day to Malmaison to see Josephine. Although the weather was very
cold, he would not enter the house but contented himself
by walking in the grounds with her, shaking her hand when
they met and doing the same when he left an hour later.

He wrote to her as soon as he returned to the Trianon:

*My dear, I found you to-day weaker than you ought to be.
You have shown courage; it is necessary that you should
maintain it and not give way to doleful melancholy. You must
be contented to take special care of your health, which is so
precious to me. If you are attached to me and if you love me
you should show strength of mind and force yourself to be happy.
You cannot question my constant and tender friendship and
you would know, very imperfectly, all the affection I have for you
if you imagined I can be happy if you are unhappy and contented
if you are ill at ease.*

Adieu, dear; sleep well. Dream that I wish it.

He wrote to her again on December 20th:

*I have just received your letter. Savary tells me that you are
always crying: that is not well. . . . I shall come and see you
when you tell me you are reasonable and that your courage
has the upper hand.*

On December 25th Josephine, accompanied by Hortense,

went to dinner at the Trianon. Napoleon wrote the next day:

> Trianon, Tuesday,
> 26th. December, 1809
>
> *My dear, I lay down after you left me yesterday. I am going to Paris. I wish to hear you are cheerful. I shall come to see you during the week.*

The following day he wrote from Paris:

> *I have been thoroughly tired in revisting the Tuileries: the great palace seemed empty to me, and I felt lost in it.*

> January 5th, 1810
>
> *It is a long time since I heard from you. . . . Adieu dear, keep well and never doubt my affection.*

> January 10th, 1810
>
> *I long to come to Malmaison, but you must really show fortitude and self-restraint. . . . Never doubt the depth of my feelings for you; you would be unjust and unfair if you did.*

> January 17th, 1810
>
> *I want badly to see you, but I must have some assurance that you are strong and not weak; I, too, am rather like you, and it makes me frightfully wretched.*

Despite Napoleon's constant enquiries and the considerable number of letters which he wrote to her about her health and welfare, Josephine was greatly alarmed to learn from reliable friends that he was becoming exasperated at this ghost of his past life.

'He intends,' they told her, 'to find some excuse to banish you from the country.'

Some of Josephine's old spirit returned when she heard this rumour. She demanded in a personal note to Napoleon that she should be allowed to live in Paris for a time to disprove the cruel rumours that were being spread.

Whether Napoleon had really intended to get her out of the way or not is a matter for argument.

Josephine used it to press for her return to Paris and she sent Eugène to Napoleon with a doleful story of loneliness and ill health.

Napoleon realised all too well that if Josephine was in Paris all his enemies would congregate in her house. He tried to buy her off.

> *Sunday, 8 p.m., 1810*
>
> *I was very glad to see you yesterday; I feel what charms your society has for me.*
>
> *To-day I walked with Estève. I have allowed £4,000 for 1810, for the extraordinary expenses at Malmaison. You can therefore do as much planting as you like; you will distribute that sum as you may require. I have instructed Estève to send £8,000 the moment the contract for the Maison Julien shall be made. I have ordered them to pay for your parure of rubies, which will be valued by the Department, for I do not wish to be robbed by jewellers. So, there goes the £16,000 that this may cost me.*
>
> *I have ordered them to hold the million which the Civil List owes you for 1810 at the disposal of your man of business, in order to pay your debts.*
>
> *You should find in the coffers of Malmaison twenty to twenty-five thousand pounds; you can take them to buy your plate and linen.*
>
> *I have instructed them to make you a very fine porcelain service; they will take your commands in order that it may be a very fine one.*
>
> *Napoleon*

Josephine thought it a feeble idea to spend good money on paying her debts, but she was far more worried at being confined to Malmaison or, worse still, Navarre.

Napoleon drove out to see her on January 18th and she

pleaded with him to allow her to return to Paris. No sooner had he left than she learnt he had finally decided to banish her to Navarre.

'I would rather die than consent to such treatment,' she cried and fainted into the arms of her ladies-in-waiting.

Napoleon was informed and wrote angrily:

I hear you are making yourself miserable. This is too bad. You have no confidence in me and all the rumours that are being spread excite you. This is not knowing me, Josephine. I am much annoyed, and if I do not find you cheerful and contented I shall scold you right well.

After another visit to Josephine, he wrote:

I have had all your affairs looked after here and ordered that everything be brought to the Elysée-Napoleon.

Josephine, thrilled and delighted, wrote him a letter warm with gratitude to which he replied:

Your letter to hand. I will see you at the Elysée and shall be very happy to see you oftener, for you know how I love you.

Josephine found, however, that it was a hollow victory. Napoleon had given orders that she was to be left alone and he was obeyed. Nobody called and she was not invited anywhere.

All she learnt from the servants and lesser officials was of Napoleon's plans for his marriage with Princess Marie Louise of Austria.

So persistent were the stories that Josephine took the almost unbelievable course of encouraging the idea. She let the Austrian Embassy know that she was wholly in favour of the marriage and insinuated that she had advised Napoleon to go through with it.

Napoleon, however, had not the slightest intention of allowing Josephine to upset his bride by her presence or her

155

intrigues. He knew only too well what Josephine's influence over him could do. He sent an official to her to say that it was his command that she should return with the least possible delay to the Château of Navarre. Although it was only sixty miles from Paris it was far enough, during winter time, to keep her out of harm's way and yet near enough for Napoleon to supervise her activities.

Josephine managed to delay her departure for some time largely on account of the excellent reason that the place was half in ruins and very poorly furnished. Repairs were hastily put in hand but it was not until March that Napoleon was able to issue a definite instruction that she was to go there on the 25th of the month and stay there at least until the end of April.

Even so, she managed to defy the Emperor and was still at Malmaison on March 27th. The next day she departed without any warning to her friends and with the knowledge of only her personal servants.

The celerity with which she eventually went indicated that Napoleon must have sent what amounted to an ultimatum. He had reason enough for this because Princess Marie Louise had on that day arrived at Courcelles.

Napoleon went to meet her and rode in her carriage as far as Compiègne, where they stayed the night. Napoleon consummated the union then and there as a preliminary to the civil and religious ceremonies arranged for April 1st and 2nd.

A good many of the ladies of Josephine's household who remained behind at Malmaison transferred on the following day to that of Marie Louise. Josephine's stay at Navarre was a desperately unhappy one. A horde of men and women who had called themselves her friends hastily left her to her fate and in an April which was unseasonably cold and miserable she spent a ghastly time in a house where the wind howled through cracked and ill-fitting windows, the fires refused to burn the sodden logs and water dripped from the ceilings.

The handful of women who remained loyal to Josephine

started bickering with the carefully chosen new ones which Napoleon sent to form her household.

Of masculine company there was really none except that the almost senile Bishop of Evreux used to amble round in the evening to talk with her and persuade her to play his favourite game of backgammon.

So exasperated did Josephine become with conditions at Navarre that she wrote to Napoleon explaining that the place was scarcely habitable and requesting permission to return to Malmaison for a few days and proceed from there to a spa.

Napoleon sent no reply.

Angrily, Josephine asked her son Eugène to approach Napoleon in person and repeat the request. Eugène, who always had a way with him when obtaining favours from his stepfather, brought back the message that she could do as she suggested.

This off-hand treatment made Josephine certain that what she had already heard was true, that Marie Louise was jealous of her and was trying to get her banished to Italy.

Furiously, and at the same time with despair in her heart, she sat down and wrote to Napoleon:

Navarre, April 18, 1810

Sire,

  I have received by my son the assurance that your Majesty consents to my return to Malmaison, and grants to me the advances asked for in order to make the Château of Navarre habitable. This double favour, Sire, dispels to a great extent the uneasiness, nay, even the fears, which your Majesty's long silence inspired. I was afraid that I might be entirely banished from your memory; I see that I am not. I am therefore less wretched to-day, and even as happy as henceforward it will be possible for me to be.

  I shall go at the end of the month to Malmaison, since your Majesty sees no objection to it. But I ought to tell you, Sire, that I should not so soon have taken advantage of the latitude which your Majesty left me in this respect had the house at

Navarre not required, for my health's sake and that of my household, repairs which are urgent. My idea is to stay at Malmaison a very short time; I shall soon leave it in order to go to the waters. But while I am at Malmaison your Majesty may be sure that I shall live there as if I were a thousand leagues from Paris. I have made a great sacrifice, Sire, and every day I realise more its full extent. Yet that sacrifice will be, as it ought to be, a complete one on my part. Your Highness, amid your happiness, shall be troubled by no expression of my regret.

I shall pray unceasingly for your Majesty's happiness, perhaps even I shall pray that I may see you again; but your Majesty may be assured that I shall always respect it in silence, relying on the attachment that you had for me formerly. I shall call for no new proof, I shall trust to everything from your justice and your heart.

I limit myself to asking from you one favour, it is that you will deign to find a way of sometimes convincing both myself and my entourage that I have still a small place in your memory and a great place in your esteem and friendship. By this means, whatever happens, my sorrows will be mitigated without, as it seems to me, compromising that which is of permanent importance to me—the happiness of your Majesty.

Josephine

Napoleon, as usual when challenged by Josephine, capitulated. He wrote in reply:

Compiègne, April 21, 1810

My Dear,

  I have yours of April 18. It is written in a bad style. I am always the same; people like me do not change. I don't know what Eugène has told you. I have not written to you because you have not written to me, and my sole desire is to fulfil your slightest inclination.

I see with pleasure that you are going to Malmaison and that you are contented; as for me, I shall be so, likewise, on hearing news from you and in giving you my news. I say no more about

*it until you have compared this letter with yours, and after that
I will leave you to judge which of us two is the better friend.
Adieu, dear; keep well and be just, for your sake and mine.*

Napoleon

Josephine's reply was warm, generous and characteristic.

*A thousand, thousand loving thanks for not having forgotten
me. My son has just brought me your letter. With what im-
petuosity I read it, and yet I took a long time over it, for there
was not a word which did not make me weep, but these tears
were very pleasant ones. I have found my whole heart again—
such as it will always be. There are affections which are life
itself and which can only end with it.*

*I was in despair to find my letter of the 19th had displeased
you. I do not remember the exact expressions, but I know what
torture I felt in writing it—the grief at having no news from you.*

*I wrote you on my departure from Malmaison, and since then
how often have I wished to write to you! But I appreciated the
causes of your silence and feared to be importunate with a letter.
Yours has been the true balm for me. Be happy, be as much
so as you deserve; it is my whole heart speaks to you. You have
also just given me my share of happiness, and a share which
I value the most, for nothing can equal, in my estimation, a
proof that you still remember me.*

*Adieu, dear; I thank you as affectionately as I shall always
love you.*

Josephine

There were, of course, many people only too anxious to
visit Josephine and give her details and descriptions of the
splendour of the wedding ceremony, to eulogise Marie
Louise's beauty and youth and to describe Napoleon's
happiness in his wife.

Josephine listened attentively and made no comments
beyond the conventional ones that she hoped the couple
would be very happy.

The complete absence of any evidence of jealousy on Josephine's part was not reflected in the attitude of Marie Louise. The rumours of her hostility were not exaggerated. She soon showed that she was considerably disturbed by the thought of the proximity to Paris of her husband's first wife.

She petulantly attempted to get Napoleon to countermand the decree that Josephine should remain Empress Queen Crowned and asked that she should be reduced to a Duchess. She also asked that Josephine should be exiled from the country or, at least, be made to live in a far more distant part of France than Malmaison or Navarre.

Napoleon would not hear of this. As a matter of fact, he talked over with Eugène a programme for Josephine for at least a year ahead, trying to make her life interesting by a tour of France and Italy with rest periods in between at Malmaison, Navarre or Plombières.

There was no suggestion that these considerable journeyings were motivated by desire to get Josephine out of the way. On the contrary, Napoleon expressed a hope that she would in time come to love the Château of Navarre once it had been put in a decent state of habitation.

On June 13th, after he had completed a tour with Marie Louise through Northern France and Belgium, he announced that he intended to visit Josephine at Malmaison. He made this and several other visits secretly without the knowledge of his wife.

The meetings were exciting to them both and Josephine always managed to control her emotion although invariably there was an outburst of crying after he had gone. The visits to Malmaison became so frequent that they could not, of course, remain secret from Marie Louise. She was livid with fury and treated Napoleon to such an exhibition of hysterical jealousy that he thought it advisable to cease the visits. He also rather half-heartedly promised not to write so often to his former wife.

It was easy for him to do this at this moment for Josephine

was just about to start on a tour, having decided to go to
Aix-les-Bains instead of Plombières. There she thought that
Hortense, now very ill from the disgusting treatment she
suffered at the hands of her husband, might join her and regain
her health.

At the spa during that summer Josephine did her best to
enjoy heself, often bathing in the lake of Geneva, going for
long excursions into the mountains and organising gay
parties in the evenings. Among the lesser lights of the nobility
of the nearby countries there were many who were glad to
entertain and visit the ex-Empress of France.

In a letter to Hortense she said:

*I have not heard from the Emperor; but I thought I ought to
prove to him the interest I have in the Empress's pregnancy. I
have just written to him on the subject. I hope that this proceeding will put him at his ease and that he will be able to speak
to me about it with a confidence as great as my attachment
to him.*

When the news arrived that Marie Louise was pregnant,
Josephine redoubled her amusements as if to conceal the
hurt in her heart. When she was not with a crowd of people
Josephine went back to her old pastime of 'telling the cards'.
They invariably foretold disaster and this made her agitated
and uneasy.

But the fact that Marie Louise had so quickly and easily
achieved what she herself had been unable to do in fifteen
years was eventually too much for her resolve to put a good
face on things. Instead of going on the projected tour of
Italy, she returned to Navarre. She sent a request to Napoleon
that she might spend twenty-four hours at Malmaison to
collect various personal possessions, and this permission was
granted.

The twenty-four hours extended to three weeks. Marie
Louise began to indulge in tantrums and outbursts of crying
about Josephine's presence so near to Paris and Napoleon,

alarmed that she might miscarry, sent a peremptory order to Josephine to leave for Navarre immediately.

Even so she defied him and it was not until three days later that she set off. There in the Château which Napoleon had excellently repaired as he had promised, Josephine prepared to spend the winter and to await the news of the birth of an heir to the throne of France.

13

No woman can await the birth of her husband's child by another woman with equanimity.

In the vast and ugly rooms of Navarre Josephine pondered on the emotional factors of the past few months. Noting both the similarities to, and the contrasts with, her own marriage and that of Marie Louise she may have found a gleam of humour in the haste with which Napoleon had consummated the union with his new wife before the marriage ceremony.

She could look back to precisely the same sequence of events and she could not help but wonder if their first night of love had been as wildly thrilling as when Napoleon had been excited to madness by his passion for her.

The sense of inferiority and failure which Josephine had always felt in never being able to bear a child for Napoleon was a more bitter sensation now than it had ever been.

Her own ignorance, and the rudimentary knowledge of gynaecology of the medical profession of the period, left only a resigned acceptance of the facts of the case: she had borne children before she met Napoleon. He had fathered children by other women. Therefore she was the culprit.

Morbid thoughts of this kind were reasonable enough in a woman of forty-seven, pyschologically disturbed by the menopause, conscious of the signs of dying sexual attractiveness. It was hard to be paraded before the whole world as a wife who had failed her husband and his people.

It speaks volumes for Josephine's generous nature, completely free from the desire for vengeance, that she genuinely worried about Marie Louise's pregnancy. She dreaded that she might hear of a miscarriage or still-birth. Such mishaps were of course common enough at the time. The birth of a live healthy child and the survival of the mother were not much more than a fifty-fifty chance even for the cosseted and cared-for consorts of Emperors.

A less magnaminous woman than Josephine could have privately hoped that some such tragedy would occur. But Josephine was of better metal. After so much sacrifice and misery she longed for Napoleon to attain his desire.

Plenty of the sycophants who had deserted her and flocked to the circle around Marie Louise were already regretting the change. The new Empress was small-minded and ill-tempered. The combination could be dangerous, for Marie Louise could never appreciate the inevitability of conspiracies of Court politics, and her emotional instability sent her running hot-foot to Napoleon for redress and comfort whenever she felt herself slighted.

If Josephine deliberately resorted to fainting fits to obtain her ends Marie Louise indulged in bouts of weeping because she could not help it. With a man as insensitive as Napoleon to women's character these occasions were numerous.

When he happened to be driving with his expectant wife and they approached Malmaison his offer to show her the place was undoubtedly so that she could admire the gardens. They had been laid out with Dutch bulbs and English roses by Josephine with consummate artistry.

Napoleon was genuinely bewildered when Marie Louise began wailing the moment he had made the suggestion. When he demanded what was wrong she started to writhe and roll about the coach to such an extent that he imagined that she was in premature labour.

This story was in time retailed to Josephine as a piece of amusing gossip by malicious courtiers. But, to her, it was the alarming indication that Marie Louise was not the tough resilient type to overcome the risks of pregnancy. Instead of joining in the laughter she begged her informers somehow to persuade Napoleon not to revive the past with such inappropriate actions.

On another occasion Josephine regretted her own carelessness. She was always losing things, and she was as carefree with her possessions as she was with the bills for payment that accompanied them. It was a byword that wherever she had been staying handkerchiefs, trinkets, private letters and pieces of jewellery would be scattered around.

Servants were specially chosen for their honesty so as to avoid trouble when they were tempted to filch the articles they picked up.

A special search was made in the Tuileries after the divorce so as to clear out every memento of Josephine. One thing was overlooked: a jewel-encrusted miniature of her painted soon after her marriage.

Marie Louise found it in the crevice of a sofa in her bedroom which had, of course, been Josephine's.

Napoleon found her sprawled on the sofa, crying hysterically. After a time he saw that she was clutching something in her hand. He prised her fingers open and saw the miniature.

'Who gave you that?' he demanded angrily.

'I found it in the sofa,' she wailed.

Napoleon was furious, believing that someone had purposely put the miniature there in order to upset Marie Louise. He may have been right.

Josephine wondered if this was so too. But her magnanimity influenced her to confess that she had not seen the trinket for years and that she vaguely remembered an evening when Napoleon and she had been sitting together. He was looking at the portrait and she had pulled it away from him and begged him admire the real face and not the replica. . . .

'It was wrong of me to forget that someone else might find it and dislike it,' she said, not seeming to appreciate the basic absurdity of a wife taking precautions against upsetting a possible successor ten or fifteen years later.

Navarre was now slightly more comfortable thanks to the alterations authorised by Napoleon, and much more homely, thanks to Josephine's extravagant furnishings.

Her life, as Napoleon's spies reported, was blameless—almost sedate. She took to lying in bed in the mornings, not having breakfast until eleven o'clock. She would later walk round the gardens or, if it was wet, drive through the countryside. Dinner in the late afternoon was an elaborate meal, with footmen in the Imperial livery standing behind each chair. In the evenings she did embroidery and listened to her reader.

Few men were among her guests. Josephine was getting more and more pleasure in having young and pretty women around her. She found their frothy and inconsequential conversation more entertaining than the carping and malicious political gossip of the women of her own generation.

She was as generous as ever. On New Year's Day, 1811, she organised a lottery of jewels and distributed them according to the dicates of a spinning wheel.

Her charm and hospitality steadily attracted a growing number of guests. Some were of sufficient political importance to start the tongues wagging in Paris. But the innuendo that 'the Navarre Party', as Josephine's allies came to be known, were being cunningly manipulated for her own ends was quite untrue.

Even her friends misjudged her selfless interest in the welfare of Marie Louise. When it was known that the baby was expected in mid-March the Mayor of Evreux arranged a banquet. It was ostensibly to celebrate the end of Lent, but was, in fact, to give their well-loved and distinquished resident a social occasion to offset the nation-wide celebrations which Napoleon had ordered to be held when the birth was announced.

To the Mayor's surprise Josephine did not arrive, sending some of her ladies instead. Napoleon had sent her word that the birth of the baby was imminent, and he had promised to despatch a messenger with the news immediately he had any. Josephine did not intend to be out when the messenger arrived.

Always at hand were two gifts, wrapped and complete with

the message of congratulation. One was a diamond pin worth 12,000 francs for a boy; the other, a smaller pin worth 5,000 francs for a girl.

The news arrived at eleven o'clock the night after the banquet—March 20th, 1811. Later that morning Eugène appeared full of information about the child's appearance and good health. He also added some pithy comments about the ill-concealed fury of Napoleon's sisters when they heard that the baby was a boy. Josephine knew full well the venomous jealousy of the sisters-in-law. She wondered if Marie Louise had been able to deal with them as efficiently as she had.

She promptly wrote a letter of congratulation to Napoleon, deeming it wiser not to send even a formal note to his wife. She included a sentence or two about her own son. She could not help hoping that the arrival of an heir would not make Napoleon forget his regard for Eugène.

Napoleon replied:

Paris, March 22nd, 1811

My Dear, I have your letter. I thank you for it. My son is fat, and in excellent health. I trust he may continue to improve. He has my chest, my mouth, and my eyes. I hope he may fulfil his destiny. I am always well pleased with Eugène; he has never given me the least anxiety.

Napoleon

Josephine undoubtedly experienced a vicarious pleasure in the birth of Napoleon's son. Despite eye trouble, caused, her doctors said, by her constant crying, she began to indulge in a much gayer existence.

She spent a month at Malmaison when the spring flowers there were at their best, and returned to Navarre in time for her forty-eighth birthday. The celebrations were on a scale which locally eclipsed those to celebrate the birth of Marie Louise's son. Evreux was illuminated, the townsfolk presented Josephine with a marble bust of herself and at the Château there was an Arcadian party with everyone dressed as peasants.

Josephine was in better health but she was growing fat. She had worried consulations with her doctor but he could suggest nothing which was any help.

In September she returned to Malmaison where she was to look after her two grandchildren while their mother, Hortense, was away. Josephine spoiled the children, particularly the younger, Napoleon Louis, whom she always called Oui-Oui. They were the first words the child had said and which he proudly repeated whatever was said to him.

There were always guests at Malmaison. Josephine's dinner parties, and even her breakfasts, regularly had more numerous and more distinguished guests than at the similar occasions in the apartments of Marie Louise. Delighted, despite her innermost wishes to efface herself, at this regard Josephine began to spend money like water, both on entertainment and on herself.

She was feminine enough to enjoy choosing more of her famous deceptively plain gowns. She now had a new one almost every day and received many compliments which managed at the same time to disparage the pretty-pretty and ostentatious gowns of her successor in the Imperial household.

Marie Louise complained vociferously to Napoleon about the rival Court, and, mean-minded, found the chink in Napoleon's armour which repelled most of her other attacks on Josephine. This was his dislike of her extravagance.

Napoleon called for detailed accounts of Josephine's and was horrified at what he discovered.

He wrote sharply to Josephine on August 25th, 1811:

Put some order into your affairs. Spend only £60,000 [a year] and save as much every year. This will make a reserve of £600,000 in ten years for your grandchildren. It is pleasant to be able to give them something and be helpful to them. Instead of that I hear you have debts, which would be really too bad. Look after your affairs and don't give to everyone who wants to help himself. If you wish to please me, let me hear that you

*have accumulated a large fortune. Consider how ill I must think
of you that you, with £120,000 a year, are in debt.*

This, however, had no effect except to send Josephine to
bed in tears. In November he tried other tactics and wrote
to Count Mollien, the Minister of the Public Treasury:

Wesel, 1st, November, 1811

*The Crown Treasury has advanced a sum of several hundred
thousand francs owed by M. Pierlot to the Empress Josephine and
Queen Hortense. Please let me know when th settlement of M.
Pierlot's affairs will enable this amount to be repaid to the
Crown Treasury.*

*It would be a good plan it you would privately send for the
Empress Josephine's steward, and make him understand that
not a penny will be paid him except upon proof that he has no
outstanding debts. I will stand no nonsense about this. The
steward's own property must be the guarantee of his good
faith. You will therefore notify him that, as from 1st January
next, no payment will be made to you, or to the Crown Treasury,
except upon his certification, secured upon his own property, that
there are no debts.*

*I am informed that the expenditure on the Empress's house-
hold is hopelessly extravagant. See the steward about this.
Find out what the position is as regards payments in cash. It
is absurd that, in place of the saving of two millions that the
Empress was to have made, there should still be debts unpaid.
You should have no difficulty in getting the steward to tell
you about all this, and in making him see that he himself might
be in a very awkward situation.*

*Arrange for a personal interview with the Empress Josephine.
Make her understand that I hope her establishment will be
managed more economically, and that, if it is not, she will
incur my extreme displeasure. The Empress Louise has only
100,000 crowns; she pays her bills every week: and she goes
without frocks, and stints herself in various ways, rather than
run into debt.*

It is therefore my intention that, as from 1st January next, not a penny more shall be paid on account of the Empress Josephine's establishment, except upon a certificate from the steward saying that there are no debts. Look into the accounts for 1811, and the estimate of expenditure for 1812. The latter ought not to exceed one million. If too many horses are being kept, some must be got rid of. The Empress has children and grandchildren. She ought to be saving up, so as to be able to help them, instead of running up bills.

You must not make any more payments to Queen Hortense, either under the head of 'apanage' or of 'Timber', without asking me first. Have a talk with her steward too. Tell him her establishment must be properly managed: not only must there be no debts, but also all expenditure must be carefully regulated.

Josephine had her own ideas for economising. She thought it would be cheaper in the long run to pull down Malmaison and build a more modern and a trifle smaller house in its place. To get the money for this she suggested that Napoleon should buy the Elysée Palace from her.

He was ready to consider this peculiar selling back of a generous gift because Marie Louise was always grumbling about 'that woman' having such a splendid residence in the capital. Unfortunately Napoleon's idea was to pay Josephine in kind and not in cash. He gave her the palace of Laeken outside Brussels in exchange for the Elysée. The proposition became in effect an Imperial order and Josephine had to accept the deeds of Laeken and yield the Elysée. She never set foot in Laeken.

There had been one or two formal meetings with Napoleon over this business and Josephine took the opportunity to beg permission to see little Napoleon, already King of Rome.

Napoleon had to confess that his wife would never countenance it, but he suggested that if Josephine really wanted to see the child—and he himself was anxious for her to do so—she should meet him by accident.

'Every afternoon his nurse takes him out for a drive and they rest while my son is fed and goes to sleep at the Pavilion de Holland in the Bois de Boulogne,' he explained. 'On Monday next week I will accompany him. You can arrive at the Pavilion about three.'

Josephine was there to the minute. She picked the baby up in her arms and said in a broken voice:

'Ah, dear child! Some day, perhaps, you may know how much I have paid for your existence.'

Napoleon, greatly affected by the scene, and fearing that it had done more harm than good, gently told Josephine to give the child back to the nurse, adding:

'I think it would be better for all concerned, my dear, if you went now. I'll arrange for you to see my son again some time.'

Josephine unwillingly handed the child over. She took a step forward to embrace Napoleon, but he turned away, later formally kissing her on the cheek as a gesture of dismissal.

'Next week perhaps?' Josephine begged.

Napoleon nodded.

But by the following week Napoleon was heading east in preparation for his disastrous campaign against Russia. The meeting in the Bois de Boulogne, with Marie Louise's child sleeping in Josephine's arms, was the last occasion they ever saw or spoke to one another.

14

'What,' asked Josephine, 'will become of us if he is beaten?'

The unconquerable Napoleon was no longer invincible. The signs were there for all to see after his disastrous attempt to bring Russia to her knees.

In times of crisis Josephine was really the only person to whom Napoleon could turn in safety. Marie Louise proved absolutely useless in giving him either advice, comfort or encouragement. In February, 1814, when France was menaced on every side by her enemies, Napoleon thought longingly of Eugène and his still formidable army in Italy. It was hurtful to his pride to send an appeal for aid and he hoped that Eugène might offer voluntarily.

To achieve this there was only one thing to do and that was to write to Josephine and explain what he wanted.

Immediately Josephine sent a letter to her son:

Do not lose an instant, my dear Eugène, whatever may be the obstacles, to comply with the Emperor's orders. He has written to me on this subject. . . . France above all! France has need of all her children. Come, then, my dear son, hasten: never could your zeal so well serve the Emperor as now. Every moment is precious. . . .

Adieu, my dear Eugène, I have only time to embrace you and to repeat: Come as quickly as possible.

A temporary turn in the misfortunes of Napoleon enabled him to let Eugène know that his help was not wanted at the moment when the latter was preparing to fulfil his mother's request and hurry by forced marches to his stepfather's side.

Josephine took the easy way out from the unbearable frustration of being unable to help by launching into an unceasing round of gaiety. She blithely spent money as if everything was fine in the world and not a cloud existed in the spring skies over Paris.

Although Josephine was literally terrified that even now she should anger Napoleon by her extravagance, the mania for frittering away money still gripped her.

At Malmaison she wanted to initate the English style of garden—a pursuit which was hardly diplomatic at a time when there was so much hostility about England and all things English. But she persisted in her plans and not only did she manage to buy large quantities of English plants, but she changed the formal rectangles of the typical French pleasure garden with its straight paths and beds laid out with geometrical precision to the carefree 'natural' style of England.

The botanical gardens were devoted to rare plants from all corners of the world—obtained during war-time at fantastic expense. She paid 4,000 francs (£160) for a single tulip bulb, but she undoubtedly contributed much to the science of horticulture, the benefits of which remain in France today.

In the enormous hot-houses, which consumed unheard-of quantities of fuel in winter, she attempted to re-create the tropical luxuriance of her Martinique home. She even managed to grow some sugar-cane there.

Although the land was really unsuitable, she created a sheep farm and stocked it with rare varieties of merino sheep. The dairy farm was a perfect reproduction of a Swiss farm. The men and women in charge were imported from Switzerland, given Swiss chalets to live in, and ordered always to wear Swiss national costume at their work.

Since her divorce Josephine had put on a lot of weight. Napoleon wrote in one of his letters:

They tell me you are getting as stout as a good farmer's wife from Normandy.

Such was Josephine's natural grace, however, that her increasing stoutness suited her. The Duchesse d'Abrantés, her constant companion, despite a certain rivalry between them, said that Josephine's physical maturity and increased weight improved her face, eradicating the lines and giving her an almost jolly appearance.

With her innate good taste in clothes she carefully altered her styles to set off her plumpness rather than making any attempt to disguise it.

Years later, Napoleon at St. Helena said to Barry O'Meara:

'Josephine was grace personified. Everything she did was with a peculiar grace and delicacy. I never saw her act negligently during the whole time we lived together. She was the goddess of the toilet, all the fashions originated with her; everything she put on appeared elegant.'

So frequent were the stories and reports lauding her appearance that Marie Louise went to the same dressmakers and milliners. The result was not a happy one for the young Empress. Her own taste was atrocious, while the craftswomen who delighted themselves in catering for Josephine made only half-hearted, and sometimes deliberately untasteful, efforts on behalf of Marie Louise.

Josephine's extravagance appeared worse than it actually was. Tradesmen put in bills for bigger quantities of goods than they had actually supplied and doubled the prices of those she, in fact, had. Thus a bill for thirty-eight hats in one month did not infer, as it appeared to do, that she wore more than one new hat a day.

She used scent with discretion but a bill for 800 francs from a perfumer was proof of the man's talents in fraud more than his skill with distillations.

One room at Malmaison was filled with memories of the past. It was the study where Napoleon had sat for an hour or two on the last occasion that he had visited the house before the divorce. The history book which he had been reading lay open on the desk just as he had left it. The pen he had been using was beside the ink well, which was regularly cleaned and

174

refilled with precisely the quantity of fluid that had been in it on that day.

A map of Europe on which he had marked lines of proposed strategy remained on the wall. The clothes he had taken off when he arrived lay in a crumpled pile on a chair and the fresh ones ready for him in the drawers and cupboards were constantly laundered and pressed. A small camp bed in the corner of the room which he had used for one of his famous lapses into the deep sleep lasting a matter of a few minutes was kept aired and ready.

Few people were ever allowed to see this room but Josephine herself visited it daily, and sometimes spent a considerable time inside. When she emerged her face showed that she had been crying.

Weeping there she would remember how angry she had been when Napoleon would shoot the wild-fowl and rare birds, with which she had stocked her ponds, from the window.

Once he had invited several generals to breakfast and during the meal he asked his guests to have a shot from the windows at the deer. Josephine was incensed.

'What!' she cried. 'Shoot at this time of year? What are you thinking about? All the animals are with young: it's not the season for shooting.'

'Oh well,' Napoleon had replied sulkily, 'I see we must give it up. Everything is prolific here except Madame!'

She had been hurt at the time and she cried again now to think how different everything might have been if only she could have had a child.

But there were happy memories too. The time when, after his marriage to Marie Louise, Napoleon had come to Malmaison and, taking Josephine in his arms, had said:

'My darling Josephine, I have always loved you; I love you still!'

Josephine would recount this story over and over again to her friends, adding:

'He said that all his efforts were useless. To love me and to die; that is his fate.'

Although history was to make it impossible for any further meetings after that 'accidental' rendezvous in the Bois de Boulogne, Josephine dreamt that the day might come when, Marie Louise having fulfilled her duty and given him a son, Napoleon would return to her.

When the dark clouds of disaster gathered Josephine's dream changed and she imagined that, with the whole world against him, he might find a haven at Malmaison and in her arms.

It was not to be. Events moved so fast that defeat came to France before Napoleon could reach his capital.

On March 25th, Napoleon's father-in-law, the Emperor of Austria, announced that he regarded the continuance of Bonaparte as Emperor of France as hostile to the peace of Europe.

Marie Louise had been appointed Regent of France while Napoleon was on active service and Josephine was horrified to think that a king could declare war on his own daughter.

Typically, Josephine made no protest or complaint, even to her intimate friends, at the supine way in which Marie Louise accepted the situation. But she made up her mind to go to the Tuileries to see if she could help the new Empress. Marie Louise had always let it be known that she never wanted to set eyes on her predecessor but this was an extreme emergency and Josephine had never been petty-minded.

She heard what news there was from Hortense who spent the last few evenings before the fall of Paris with Marie Louise.

Joseph and Lucien were planning to remove the Empress and her son—the King of Rome—from Paris, but Hortense advised her not to go.

'At least, sister, remember that you lose your crown!' she said.

'Perhaps you are right,' Marie Louise answered, 'but thus it has been decided and if the Emperor reproaches anyone it will not be me.'

But even Hortense realised nothing could be gained by staying when the Bonapartes all left amid booing and ugly gestures from the crowds. As the shopkeepers tore down the signs and emblems of Napoleon from their doors she sent an urgent messenger to Josephine to tell her to hurry to Navarre.

Josephine who had been making bandages with her ladies, wrote miserably:

> *March 28th*
>
> *My dear Hortense, I had courage up to the moment when I received your letter. I cannot think without anguish that I am separating myself from you, God knows for how long a time. I am following your advice; I shall leave tomorrow for Navarre. I have here only a guard of sixteen men, and all are wounded. I will keep them, but really I have no need of them. I am so unhappy at being separated from my children that I am indifferent to my fate. I am troubled only about you. Try to send me news, to keep me informed of your plans, and to tell me whither you go. I shall at least try to follow you from afar. Good-bye, my dear daughter; I embrace you tenderly.*

Miserable and helpless, half-believing a rumour that Napoleon had been killed, and yearning for someone in authority who could tell her how best she could help the Emperor if he was still alive, the old fears now gripped Josephine completely.

She was not by instinct a courageous woman and yet, despite her terrors, she forced herself to search in the rooms at Malmaison and in innumerable drawers for money. Somehow or other she gathered together 50,000 francs. She got her maid to sew her best diamonds and pearls inside her petticoat. She insisted on loading her carriage with her jewellery cases, pictures, miniatures and *objets d'art* until the driver warned her that there would be no room for herself.

Eventually in pouring rain the sorry little procession started off. All the countryside was in a complete panic, with rumours of the savagery of the enemy now in control of the capital spreading like wildfire.

No one troubled to tell Josephine—and probably no one on the road knew it—that Napoleon was alive and had reached Fontainebleau.

Fear was rampant everywhere. When a nervous soldier who had been in the retreat from Moscow saw a group of horsemen come over a hill some miles to the east he shouted: 'The Cossacks!'

Josepine opened the carriage door and jumped out before the driver could rein in his horses, and started to run towards a wood. Her guards rushed after her as best they could and eventually caught her, begging her to look at the mounted group which was by this time much nearer and was clearly to be recognised as a group of refugees like themselves. Trembling and crying, Josephine was led back to the carriage and the journey resumed.

The first two days at Navarre brought the very depths of misery to her. Not only was she unaware of Napoleon's whereabouts but she was deeply worried about Hortense and Eugène and about their children.

She wrote to her daughter:

March 31st

I cannot tell you how unhappy I am. I have had courage in the painful positions in which I have found myself, I shall have it to bear the reverses of fortune. But I have not sufficient to put up with my children's absence and the uncertainty of their fate. For two days I have not ceased to shed tears. Send me news of yourself and of your children; if you have any of Eugène and his family, let me hear. I very much fear no news will come from Paris, seeing that the post from Paris to Evreux had broken down—which has led to the circulation of a lot of news. Among other things, it is asserted that the Neuilly bridge has been occupied by the enemy. This would be very near to Malmaison. . . .

On April 1st, Hortense turned up with her two sons quite

safe but with the news that Paris had surrendered and that the Emperor was still at Fontainebleau; no one knew what he was doing.

Bitterly Hortense recounted how innumerable officials and members of society were remaining in Paris and already organising a reception of welcome to the allied armies. It was nearly a week before communications between Paris, Fontainebleau and Blois were resumed.

In the early hours of the morning Josephine was awakened to learn that a courier had arrived from the Emperor. She sat up in bed and insisted that the messenger should be admitted to her bedroom immediately.

'He is alive then? Tell me!' she demanded desperately.

The courier sadly gave the news that Napoleon had abdicated and had accepted the decree of banishment to Elba.

Josephine rushed crying into Hortense's bedroom and threw herself on the bed.

'Poor, poor Napoleon! He is sent to the island of Elba! How wretched he will be! Were it not for his wife, I would go and shut myself up with him!'

Early next morning Josephine asked one of her ladies-in-waiting to go to Paris to hand a message of sympathy to the Emperor and to enquire about her son Eugène.

She had no means of knowing whether her message reached Napoleon. Probably it was intercepted by the Bourbon faction or the Allied Powers. She remained beset with anxiety and a prey to the doubts.

At last a letter, delayed by the breakdown in communications, reached Josephine from Napoleon in the middle of April. It was addressed from Fontainebleau and in it Napoleon said:

Dearest Josephine. I wrote a letter to you on the eighth but possibly you did not receive it, as hostilities continue, and it may have been intercepted. I have formed my resolve: I will not repeat what I wrote in that letter: then I complained about

179

my situation; now I congratulate myself on it. I am now free from a terrible burden. My fall was great, but at least it was useful. In my exile I shall substitute the pen for the sword. I have brought happiness to millions of my countrymen. What have they done in the end for me? They have all betrayed me. Yes, all of them. I except the good Eugène, so worthy of you and of me. Goodbye, my dearest Josephine.

P.S. I expect to hear from you at Elba. I am not feeling very well.

The letter seared into Josephine's heart. She noted the bitterness and disillusion; the bravado about being glad that it was all over.

She worried if this time his final sentence was not just his usual way of saying he was ill and forgetting it a few minutes later. She suspected that the indigestion from which he had suffered more and more frequently even before the divorce, making him adopt that characteristic pose with his hand on his abdomen inside his tunic, was an indication of some chronic ailment. She longed to be with him to make him forget the *malaise* of his body and of his soul.

Helpless to do anything, she wrote:

Sire: Only now can I estimate the complete extent of my misfortune in my union with you being legally dissolved. Now indeed do I lament that I can be no more than your friend. . . .

I have been within an ace of quitting France to follow in your footsteps, and to devote to you the remainder of a life so long made glittering by you. One reason has restrained me, and what that is you may guess.

If I learn that, contrary to all appearance, I am the only one who will fulfil her duty to you, nothing shall restrain me, and I shall come to the only place where henceforth there can be any happiness, since I shall then be able to console you.

Say but the word and I come. Adieu, Sire. Whatever I could add would be too little. No longer can words prove my love. For actions your consent is necessary.

This letter reached Napoleon on Elba but he did not reply. He was convinced that Marie Louise and his son would follow him in his exile. He wrote letter after letter and sent messengers.

Finally he wrote to the Emperor of Austria begging him to *help me in pressing forward a moment of meeting between a wife and her husband and a child with his father.*

The Emperor did not reply nor did Marie Louise answer his letters. The truth was she had already found a lover with whom she was deeply in love. He was called the Count of Niepperg and she was to bear four children by him.

15

As a woman in a state of semi-retirement Josephine presented no danger to the Allied Powers or to the Bourbons, who were now to regain the Throne of France. As a result, no objection was made to her returning to Malmaison.

Indeed, the Tsar Alexander of Russia, who had strong feelings of admiration for Josephine from all he had read about her, eagerly invited her to return so that they could meet.

In his early thirties Alexander was exceedingly handsome and extremely charming. He was vain, religious, mystic and proud. He was, at this moment, bitterly resentful and hurt that the Allies did not recognise him as the Saviour of Europe and the sole conqueror of Napoleon.

He was the type of character that Josephine understood only too well and they became close friends. What was more, Alexander constituted himself her protector. He gave her his personal guarantee of the receipt of £40,000 a year which had been provided for her in the treaty made with Napoleon by the Allies, and £16,000 to Hortense.

Little wonder that Hortense referred to him as 'Our Angel'.

Josephine was delighted to find herself treated as a woman and no longer pitied as an ex-Empress. Her position was now far less invidious than that of Marie Louise and she became rather foolish in her complete surrender to the overtures of the conquerors of France.

The Russian Royal Family visited her as well as most of the titled heads of the German principalities. Even the Emperor of Austria, who might reasonably have been regarded as the most treacherous of all who had brought about Napoleon's downfall, was offered hospitality.

Taxed about this, Josephine exclaimed with genuine mystification:

'Why shouldn't he come? It is not I who he has dethroned but his own daughter!'

Josephine's real preoccupation was to ensure Eugène's future. Not for nothing had Napoleon said: 'I win battles, Josephine wins hearts.'

So cleverly did she play upon the injured vanity of the Tsar that, to please her, he actually thought of putting Eugène on the throne of France. Unfortunately England and Austria would not hear of it.

None of this was, however, in Josephine's mind until she had discovered after every possible enquiry that there was no chance whatever of her being able to go to Elba to be with Napoleon.

Even if the Occupying Powers were to permit her to join her ex-husband, it was pointed out to her that quite a number of the members of the Bonaparte family would be going there too. Josephine did not need to be told how miserable they would make her life.

After the first few weeks of constant comings and goings of the Heads of State who were in Paris for the peace negotiations, the number of visitors at Malmaison decreased until only Alexander was a regular caller. It was a common occurrence to see the Tsar strolling in the grounds of Malmaison with Josephine on his left arm and Hortense on his right.

Alexander arranged that Hortense should be offered the Duchy of St. Leu.

In the middle of May Josephine and her daughter went to the Château for a brief holiday and to see what the place was like. Alexander promised to come over the day after they arrived.

He called on May 14th and found Josephine suffering from a heavy cold. Despite this she insisted on going out for a drive with him, and a number of other guests, to the woods of Montmorency.

A light rain was falling and Josephine's feet got very wet. By the time the party returned to the Château her cold was much worse.

She took an infusion of orange flower water which Napoleon had taught her to use and lay down until dinner time.

She was worrying all the time about her children and was convinced that the promises which had been made to them of financial assistance would never be implemented.

'Must I see my children wandering and destitute?' she asked one of her ladies. 'The idea is killing me.'

She rose and dressed herself particularly attractively for dinner in a gown which exposed most of now ample bosom.

She felt so ill however that she was unable to eat anything and after the meal was over Hortense persuaded her to go upstairs. Josephine did so but shortly before midnight she appeared again, sitting beside the Tsar while Hortense entertained the company with some singing.

On the following morning she returned to Malmaison and by the time she arrived she was feeling really desperately ill. She still refused to go to her bed and kept on sending out a stream of invitations so that there was never a breakfast or a dinner without a number of guests round her table.

Madame de Staël called on her and when she was gone Josephine said to the Duchesse de Reggio and two other guests:

'I have just had a very painful interview. Would you believe that, among other questions which Madame de Staël was pleased to put to me, she asked if I still loved the Emperor? She appeared to wish to analyse my soul in the presence of this great misfortune. I, who never ceased to love the Emperor throughout his happy days . . . is it likely that to-day I should grow cold toward him?'

On May 25th Alexander came once again as the principal guest at a dinner and dance.

Heavily made-up and wearing an even lovelier and more abbreviated gown than at the Château St. Leu, Josephine managed somehow to open the dance as Alexander's partner and afterwards to walk with him in the darkened park. He promised to dine again on the 27th.

On the morning of the 26th May Josephine awoke with a temperature and a cough which she was quite unable to control. The doctor arrived and put a blister on her chest.

The household staff were by now so alarmed at their mistress's condition that they felt it wise to inform Eugène in Paris and he came over immediately.

He recognised that his mother was very ill. Returning to the capital he let it be known in official circles that he believed Josephine was on her death-bed. The news quickly passed from mouth to mouth.

It is said that one of the people who heard it was the mysterious Scotsman with whom Josephine had had an affair so many years before in Martinique and who may have been the father of her illegitimate child. He came to see the woman whose loveliness and charm he had never forgotten and he was sitting on one side of the bed and Alexander sat on the other.

It must have been a situation which gave infinite pleasure to Josephine, who was apparently quite unaware how desperately ill she was. Alexander was so alarmed at her appearance that he sent his own doctor to see what could be done.

In conference with his French colleague, the Russian physician said that while Josephine was gravely ill he did not believe that the 'putrid fever' (diphtheria), from which she was suffering, was likely to be fatal.

But on the morning of May 29th, Whit Sunday, the waiting woman who was dozing fitfully by the bed suddenly noticed Josephine's terribly wax-like colour. She could hardly detect any sign of breathing.

She hurried away and called Eugène and Hortense. They

were unrecognised by Josephine and Eugène arranged for his mother to receive the Last Sacrament.

During the morning Josephine regained consciousness but the difficulty she had in breathing made it impossible for her to talk above a whisper. Just before noon she managed to raise her arm in the direction of her children. Eugène knelt beside her and put his arms round her. Hortense tried to do the same but fainted.

Quite clearly, in the last few seconds before death came, Josephine said slowly:

'Napoleon. . . . Elba.'

After her death her hair was cut off and given to Hortense. Her body was embalmed and lay in state so that the local people could see her. Twenty thousand filed past the open coffin. She was buried in the little church of Rueil, not far from Malmaison, the military honours being provided by a detachment of the Imperial Guards of Russia sent by Alexander who, however, did not himself attend as it would not have been correct.

Hostile to the end, members of Napoleon's family saw to it that no news of Josephine's death was given to the ex-Emperor on Elba.

Days later he was told about it when his valet, en route for Paris, bought a copy of a newspaper in Genoa and sent it to his master on Elba.

After he had read the information in the newspaper Napoleon shut himself up for the rest of the day, would see no one, and ate nothing. He never said a word to any of his relatives or his staff and he did not wear mourning—obedient to the etiquette that he could not mourn for a divorced wife while his legal wife was alive.

But after his return in triumph to Paris, one of the first things he did was to demand complete details of Josephine's last hours.

'So you let my poor Josephine die!' he said to her doctor. 'What was the cause of her illness?'

'Sire,' said the doctor, 'anxiety and sorrow.'

Napoleon went to Malmaison and shut himself in the room where Josephine had died. When he came out his face was streaked with tears.

'Good woman, good Josephine,' he whispered. 'She loved me truly.'

Bibliography

A Life of Napoleon Bonaparte, with a Sketch of Josephine, Empress of the French. Ida M. Tarbell.

Citizeness Bonaparte. Imbert de Saint Amand.

Constant, *Memoirs* (Vols. I, II, III and IV). Translated Pinkerton, 1896.

Dearest Bess. Dorothy Margaret Stuart.

Dernieres Annés de l'Impératrice Joséphine. Imbert de Saint Amand.

Dictionary of Napoleon. Richardson.

Emperor and Mystic. Francis Gribble.

Empress Josephine, Napoleon's Enchantress (Vols. I and II). Philip W. Sergeant, 1908.

Fouché, the Man Napoleon Feared. Nils Forssell.

Histoire de l'Empire. M. A. Thiers.

Histoire du Consulat. M. A. Thiers.

History of Captivity of Napoleon at St Helena (3 vols.). W. Forsyth, 1853.

History of the French Revolution. Hilaire Belloc.

History of the Peninsula War (4 vols.). Oman, 1902–1911.

History of the Revolution. M. A. Thiers.

Influences of Sea Power on the French Revolution and Empire. A. T. Mahan, 1892.

Josephine. R. Wilson, 1930.

Josephine de Beauharnais. Frederic Masson.

Josephine, Empress of the French. Frederick A. Ober.

Josephine, Wife of Napoleon. E. A. Rheinhardt, 1934.

La Cour de l'Impératrice Joséphine Imbert de Saint Amand.

La Journée de l'Impératrice Joséphine. Frederic Masson.

Le Sacre et le Couronnement de Napoléon. Frederic Masson.

Life of Napoleon. J. Holland Rose, 1905.

Life of Napoleon. W. M. Sloane, 1906.

Lucien Bonaparte et ses Memoires. Th. Jung.

Madame Bonaparte. Frederic Masson.

Madame Mère. Larey, 1892.

Memoires. Lucien Bonaparte.

Memoires. Bourienne.

Memoires. Bourienne.

Memoires. Soult, 1854.

Memoirs. Barras.

Memoirs of Chancellor Pasquier.

Memoires of Count Lavalette.

Memoirs of Napoleon, His Court, etc. (Vols. I and II). Duchesse d'Abrantés, 1836.

Memoirs of Queen Hortense. Edited Prince Napoleon.

Memorial of St. Helena. Las Cases.

Napoleon. E. Ludwig, 1927.

Napoleon Bonaparte. J. M. Thompson.

Napoleon Bonaparte and the Siege of Toulon. C. J. Fox, 1902.

Napoleon in Exile or a Voice from St Helena (2 vols.). Barry O'Meara, 1823.

Napoleon, the First Phase. O. Browning, 1905.

Napoleon and His Family. Frederic Masson.

Napoleon Immortal. James Kemble, 1959.

Napoleon, the Last Phase. Earl of Roseberry, 1900.

Napoleon the Man. R. McNair Wilson, 1927.

Napoleon et son Temps. Octave Aubrey.

Napoleonic Studies. J. H. Rose, 1904.

Napoleon's Captivity in Relation to Sir Hudson Lowe. R. C. Seaton, 1903.

Napoleon's letters to Josephine, 1796–1812. Edited and translated by H. F. Hall, 1901.

Notes and Reminiscences of a Staff Officer. Basil Jackson, 1903.

Revue de Paris. Frederic Masson.

Robespierre. Hilaire Belloc.

September Massacres. Lenotre.

Souvenirs sur Napoleon.   Comte Chaptal.
The Empress Josephine.   De Meneval.
The Empress Josephine.   R. McNair Wilson, 1932.
Une Maîtresse de Napoléon.   Hector Fleischmann.
Wife of General Bonaparte.   Joseph Turquan, 1912.
Wife of the First Consul.   Imbert de Saint Amand.

**If you would like a complete list of Arrow books
please send a postcard to
P.O. Box 29, Douglas, Isle of Man, Great Britain.**

Below are details of other books by Barbara Cartland that will be of interest:

WE DANCED ALL NIGHT

Barbara Cartland's autobiographical study of the Twenties

1919; and Barbara Cartland, leaving school, plunges into the whirl-pool of a society hectically determined to forget the horrors of the recent war. All seemed to be escapism, adventure and youthful rebellion. Nightclubs mushroomed, the Bright Young Things danced from dusk to dawn. Even today the tunes instantly recall and sum up a whole decade: the Society Balls, the excitement of the West End theatre.

And always in the thick of it, Barbara Cartland, her vivacity and energy still epitomising that of a generation. A generation active in the new developments of the Twenties: motoring, flying, wireless, medicine—many of the pioneers, personal friends of the author. Involved in many fields, Barbara Cartland's sparkling, magnetic personality shines out in this fascinating, entertaining book.

'Miss Cartland's book presents a dazzling portrait of an era where the young danced all night and the old looked on in disapproval ...'
Liverpool Daily Post

I SEARCH FOR RAINBOWS

The second volume of Barbara Cartland's autobiographical works published in paperback.

Service in the Second World War—visits to India and the Far East—the fight for proper facilities for gypsies—service on the County Council—the fight to improve the ghastly conditions in Old People's Homes—honey and vitamins, the importance of health foods: life has always been full for Barbara Cartland because she has made it full. Things don't happen to Barbara Cartland. She makes them happen. When she believes in a cause, she works for it. When she disagrees, she does not sit and grumble. She fights.

Witty, sympathetic, ever-active, outrageous sometimes, Barbara Cartland radiates energy, is a living example of everything she believes in.